For many of us, one of ⟨...⟩
team in a united cause. ⟨...⟩
its lessons don't just app⟨...⟩ ⟨...⟩⟨...⟩ trophies,
but more importantly assist us through the journey of life.

—**Gary Kirsten,** 2011 Cricket World Cup Winner as
Coach of India; Former Professional Cricket Player and
National Cricket Team Coach for South Africa

Coaches possess a tremendous amount of influence. Billy
Graham even said that a coach can have a greater influence
on the life of a young person, in just one season, than many
can in a lifetime. Shawn Brower has had that kind of influence on the lives of the young men he has coached for almost
two decades. A hugely successful coach, Brower has earned
National Coach of the Year honors twice, as well as Coach of
the Year honors in two states over multiple years. Yet with all
his success on the field, it is his godly influence and impact on
the lives of his student athletes that has resulted in a multitude
of champions in the game of life! Now Brower combines those
lessons, biblical applications, and illustrations from some of
today's great coaches and athletes in his new book *The Huddle.*
Coaches, athletes, and teams at every level need this practical
guide to use as a playbook in helping them grow and develop
relationship bonds, championship attitudes and actions based
on biblical principles, and a rock-solid spiritual foundation
that will help them win in life. This is a book I will use with
my teams, athletes, and assistant coaches!

—**Roy Heintz,** Women's Basketball Coach, University of Ala-
bama in Huntsville; Former Chaplain of Orlando Magic

For many years I have challenged teams to pursue character
above the "almighty win." Coaches and athletes aren't defined
by the scoreboard; they are known by what occurs deep in

their souls. Shawn's book provides an excellent combination of biblical truth and practical insights on how to maximize your performance on and off the field, developing the deep character issues that will benefit you all the days of your life.

—**Rod Handley,** Founder and President, Character That Counts

Building championship-caliber teams is no easy task. Dr. Brower has not only accomplished this as a coach, he has now articulated the key principles and practices in this book. Every coach and athlete at every level would benefit from this thorough, thoughtful, and practical reflection of what it really means to be a champion. Dr. Brower conveys the transcendent cause for athletics and elevates the eternal trophies above the applause gained from personal and team success.

—**Larry Taylor,** President, Prestonwood Christian Academy, Plano, Texas; Founder, Student Leadership Institute

I believe there is no higher compliment than saying that someone reflects Christ to those around them. This is what Coach does as a leader, principal, coach, father (to his kids and to me), friend, and follower of Christ. The way in which he lives with integrity, humility, and passion is infectious and points to Someone larger than himself. Coach shows me Jesus and has instilled a desire in me to follow Christ more fully. Praise the Lord for people such as Coach Brower. I would encourage *everyone* to read this book and live it out—it will lead people to the cross through its pages.

—**Roy Anderson,** Former Captain, 2011 State Championship Team, Chattanooga Christian School, Chattanooga, Tennessee

THE
HUDDLE

Becoming a Champion for Life

SHAWN BROWER

PUBLISHING
P.O. BOX 817 • PHILLIPSBURG • NEW JERSEY 08865-0817

Unless otherwise indicated, all Scripture quotations are from the HOLY BIBLE, NEW INTERNATIONAL VERSION®. NIV®. Copyright © 1973, 1978, 1984 by International Bible Society. Used by permission of Zondervan Publishing House. All rights reserved.

Scripture quotations marked (ESV) are from *ESV Bible* ® (*The Holy Bible, English Standard Version* ®). Copyright © 2001 by Crossway Bibles, a publishing ministry of Good News Publishers. Used by permission. All rights reserved.

Scripture quotations marked (NKJV) are from The Holy Bible, New King James Version. Copyright © 1979, 1980, 1982, Thomas Nelson, Inc.

Scripture quotations marked (TNIV) are taken from the *Holy Bible, Today's New International Version*®. *TNIV*®. Copyright © 2002, 2004 by International Bible Society. Used by permission of Zondervan. All rights reserved.

Italics within Scripture quotations indicate emphasis added.

ISBN: 978-1-59638-668-6 (pbk)
ISBN: 978-1-59638-669-3 (ePub)
ISBN: 978-1-59638-670-9 (Mobi)

Huddle icon © khalus/istockphoto.com

Printed in the United States of America

Library of Congress Cataloging-in-Publication Data

Brower, Shawn, 1970-
    The huddle : becoming a champion for life / Shawn Brower.
      pages cm
    Includes bibliographical references.
    ISBN 978-1-59638-668-6 (pbk.)
    1. Success. 2. Teamwork (Sports)--Psychological aspects. 3. Sports--Psychological aspects. 4. Athletes--Life skills guides. 5. Athletes--Conduct of life. 6. Leadership. I. Title.
    GV706.55.B76 2013
    796.01'9--dc23
                                    2013008148

To the CCS 2011 Men's Varsity Soccer
State Championship Team:

not because you won but because you loved well.

Your relationships defined the season and
transcended the game.

CONTENTS

Acknowledgments   7

Introduction   9

1. Perspective Changes Everything!   15

STAGE 1: PRESEASON

2. Risk Your Best   29
3. Selected   41
4. The Rules of Engagement   51
5. So These Are My Teammates?   63

STAGE 2: REGULAR SEASON

6. This *Is* "Next Year"   73
7. Pressing On   91
8. Shoot Straight with Me   101
9. Winning the Head Game   111
10. Defined in Battle   125

STAGE 3: PLAYOFFS

11. Collective Separation   139
12. Staying on Center   153
13. Victory in Defeat   161
14. The Arms around Us   171
15. Championships   181

CONTENTS

STAGE 4: POST-SEASON

16. For Life   191

STAGE 5: LEADERSHIP DEVELOPMENT

17. Captains' Club   203

    Appendix   209
    Notes   213

ACKNOWLEDGMENTS

I FIRST ACKNOWLEDGE my dear wife, who has been my best teammate for the past twenty years. Any coaching successes I have been blessed to experience are a direct result of her steady, faithful, and supportive love.

Players: A special thanks to every player who has stood with me in our team huddles. The experiences we shared and the resulting memories have been life gifts beyond imagination. I am blessed, beyond measure, because of each participating player from U-8 soccer teams to high school varsity soccer state championships. My life is richer today as a result of our time together.

Coaches: I am eternally grateful for the following men who granted me many, many hours of conversation that was not just about team tactics but offered a bond and a friendship that transcended the sport itself. Dave Murray, my college coach, inspired me to pursue excellence on the field and modeled how to pursue transformational, Christ-centered relationships with players. Doug Fleming, my assistant coach for eleven years, provided me as a young coach the richest counsel from the greatest source, as God's Word was his authority and daily sustenance. In a similar vein, John Smith, father of two former players, served as my "life coach" mentor and friend. He has been like a second father to me! Assistant coaches Gene Nelson, Bryant Black, and Doug Jipping have each offered me their camaraderie, friendship, and invaluable support. It has been a blast just "doing life together."

A special thanks to fellow coach and educational leader, and former college roommate, Jim Arnold for our modern-day

"David and Jonathan" relationship. Few relationships today remain as constant, unswerving, and genuine as I have been honored to receive from Jim. Now, twenty-four years after our first college days, I marvel that God continues to allow us to serve him together. Thank you, brother!

Sons: Joshua, Josiah, and Jakob. "Your presence, whether an infant on bus rides, or your highly energetic involvement on the sidelines, the bench, or the locker room, has always brought me great delight. It is with great fatherly pride and admiration that I watch you pursue your various athletic choices. I trust that as you train, relate and compete, you will grow in your pursuit of godly manhood and that you will forge rich and lasting relationships with the brothers in your team huddle."

INTRODUCTION

PART ONE

On Friday, May 27, at 3:30 in the afternoon, exactly one hour before my varsity men's soccer team took the field in pursuit of the Tennessee high school state soccer championship, twenty-three young men stood side by side, arm in arm together. As I looked at this tightly closed huddle, I was flooded with emotion. After this final match, six seniors would bow out, and the huddle would never be quite the same. The players also sensed the finality of this special season and this special group of guys, so I quickly reminded them that they had that last night together. As a band of brothers, they needed to rise up and run to the challenge before them. I urged them not to make this night about a game of soccer or even a state championship. Instead I encouraged them to make it about their relationships in the huddle, to make it personal. After all, this had been their perspective all year; why do anything different at this point?

As they looked around the huddle and into the eyes of their brothers, the players understood what I was saying. Many of them had been together since elementary school, had played soccer together since middle school, had been to the state tournament together three times, and were now about to play for the state championship. These guys had been living life together for a long time. They were more than a group of talented individuals. They were connected and unified in a cause and for a purpose that surpassed gold medals or a championship trophy. As I looked about the huddle, I knew

9

that regardless of outcome, this was an uncommon group of young men pursuing an uncommon achievement.

When the first whistle blew, the players ran forward with an almost reckless abandonment, refusing to back down from any challenge set before them. When the last whistle sounded, the team stormed the field, this time to hoist the championship trophy overhead and to have gold medals draped about their necks.

While the championship title was certainly a team goal, it was the outworking of the commitment and vows the players had made to each other inside that huddle. More than they played against an opponent, they played with their teammates. In those waning moments of their season, their camaraderie and brotherhood was of greatest value and significance and was the x factor that led our team to victory.

It is said that a great opponent often brings out the best in a team. Yet I would contend that the strongest opponent cannot motivate, challenge, and inspire a team to greatness as can a unified group of teammates. Deeply interwoven into the fabric of each other's lives, they are fully dedicated to each other, just like a band of brothers fighting together in the trenches.

This culture and those relationships do not happen by accident. In fact, it is extremely rare for a group of individuals to be able to unite for a common cause to the degree I have just described. But when it happens, spectators see it, other teams wish they had it, and the team that lives and experiences it will never forget it.

This is why I have written this book. In my twenty years of coaching high school athletics, I have been blessed with many talented players and successful seasons. God has allowed me to guide seven teams to the state championship title match, win four state championships titles, and hold an 80 percent winning record during my coaching tenure. However, this book is not just about winning, being the best, and raising the championship trophy—although these accomplishments provide memories for a lifetime and are worthy to pursue. This book is much more about viewing your sport(s) as a microcosm of life.

You can learn incredible lessons that will assist you as an athlete and propel your team to achieve uncommon results while simultaneously equipping you for life during and after your athletic pursuits. I hope this book serves you well by preparing you for a successful season marked by deep and lasting relationships with your teammates, growth through victories and inevitable setbacks, and assistance in making the vital connections between athletics and all of life.

PART TWO

Many respect Coach John Wooden as one of the greatest all-time coaches in any sport, as he set a blazing record of coaching the University of California, Los Angeles (UCLA) Bruins to ten National Collegiate Athletic Association (NCAA) basketball championships. The richness and goodness of the words he offered his players at the start of a new season could not be more fitting for framing the focus and message of this book. In *Wooden on Leadership*, Wooden recalls how he stood before his players and said these words at the beginning of preseason:

> We all want to be very successful, but for our success to become a reality you must first accept my concept of what success truly is. True success in basketball shouldn't be based on individual statistics or the percentage of victories, any more than success in life should be based on material possession or a position of power and prestige. Success must be based

on how close you come to reaching your own particular level of competency.

Outscoring an opponent is important, and we must give an honest effort to do that, but you must keep things in proper perspective. Our efforts on the court are only building blocks for achieving success in life, and that should be our main purpose in being here. . . .

We must not become too concerned about the things over which we have no control, but we must make every effort to utilize to the best of our ability the things over which we have control.

Everyone is different. There will always be others who are bigger or stronger, or quicker, or better jumpers, or better in some other areas, but there are other qualities in which you can be second to none.

Among these are—your dedication to the development of your own potential, your industriousness, your physical condition, your integrity, self-control, team spirit and cooperation. If you acquire and keep these traits, I can assure you that you will be successful, not just in basketball, but in life, which is of far greater importance.

Although we press to become better in our sport, something bigger and grander exists beyond athletic contests and even their best outcomes. The lessons leaping from these pages are only good if you apply them to your life. In so doing, you will reap great benefits!

If you review the table of contents you will see that this book is divided into four seasons: preseason, regular season, playoffs, and post-season. The goal is to read through each section before you enter that particular portion of your season. To maximize the return on the time you will invest in reading this book, consider reading through and answering the questions together with your teammates. In so doing, you and your team will not only have the opportunity to read, talk, and discuss the same content but also be able to apply and process areas specific to your team. Not only will your team benefit from common thinking and processing through shared experiences, but you will also have a better understanding of how to resolve areas of concern and how to be best prepared for what lies ahead in the next phase in your season.

CHAPTER ONE

PERSPECTIVE CHANGES EVERYTHING!

*"For we are God's workmanship, created in Christ
Jesus to do good works, which God prepared in
advance for us to do." —Ephesians 2:10*

HEADLINES

- Athletics cannot be separated from our faith.
- We can follow professional modern athletes of faith.
- Our perspective on faith and athletics changes everything.

LETTER FROM COACH

In January 1993, I was a senior at a Christian liberal arts college in the small town of Beaver Falls, Pennsylvania, known primarily as the hometown of National Football League (NFL) great Joe Namath. I had just finished four years of playing collegiate soccer, and the other team captain and I decided to stay fit and keep training together even though our college soccer days were through.

One Friday evening as we were working out, the athletic director came by to tell us that the gym would be closing in a few minutes because that was the policy during home basketball games. Knowing we were close to the end of our workout, we continued to lift weights. A few minutes later, the athletic director came by again and said, "All right, time to leave." Then he walked away.

Now very close to finishing, we continued to lift weights. When the director came to turn off the lights a few minutes later, we were still working out. "Hey, didn't I ask you guys to leave?" he said. "What's going on?" We stopped and left the gym, thinking very little about the incident.

On Monday morning, I went to the college mailroom to check my box. Inside was one sheet of paper from my coach with these words typed on it: "That you were asked three times to leave the gym by the athletic director is deeply concerning. Have I taught you nothing? Both of you are captains, whether in season or out, and you represented yourself, the team, and our soccer program poorly by willfully choosing to not leave the first time the athletic director spoke to you. If I have somehow taught this to you, then I have failed you greatly. Please come directly to my office!"

I immediately left the mailroom to see Coach Murray. I knew I had messed up and messed up pretty big. I walked in, and before he could say anything, I offered him a sincere, heartfelt apology for my actions and asked for forgiveness.

Twenty years later, I still have this letter. You might think it wasn't that big a deal. However, this incident was huge! It had something to do with soccer and everything to do with life. I have kept this letter as a stern reminder that my faith is always on display. I cannot separate who I am from what I do. Even though my collegiate playing days were over, my coach took the time to inseparably tie together athletics, my faith, and my life. For that lesson, I will be forever grateful.

FAITH *IS* LIFE

Why this opening story? What is the connection between athletics and life? Let me offer a simple statement and then explain. Faith *is* life. If you can understand this truth, my opening story and the rest of this book will make sense. When my coach told me I was a captain in season or out of season, that did it for me! That was it! In the same way, I am a Christian regardless of what I am doing and what I am pursuing. My faith should be evident in all aspects of my life, at all times.

We cannot hold a dualistic view of our faith that separates it from something else—in this case, athletics. We must not see faith as an add-on so that we talk about "athletics" and "faith" as if they are individual ideas that stand alone. Our faith must be tightly linked in every way to every area of life. It must permeate all areas of life so that it cannot be separated from them, just as green dye dropped into a glass of clear water changes the color of all the water.

It is important that we understand this point. It changes everything! Our highest authority, God's Word, tells us how to pursue athletics as Christians. To begin, we must recognize *who made us and how we are made.* King David says,

> For you created my inmost being;
>> you knit me together in my mother's womb.
> I praise you because I am fearfully and wonderfully made;
>> your works are wonderful,
>> I know that full well. (Ps. 139:13–14)

The prophet Isaiah recorded God's words: "Bring my sons from afar and my daughters from the ends of the earth—everyone who is called by my name, whom I created for my glory, whom I formed and made" (Isa. 43:6–7).

Not only has God fashioned and designed us, but he has *given each of us certain gifts and abilities.* The apostle Paul writes,

> There are different kinds of gifts, but the same Spirit. There are different kinds of service, but the same Lord. There are different kinds of working, but the same God works all of them in all men. (1 Cor. 12:4–6)

James adds, "Every good and perfect gift is from above, coming down from the Father of the heavenly lights, who does not change like shifting shadows" (James 1:17).

So we know God made us and gifted us . . . but for what end? Simply put—*to bring God glory!* We are made by him and *for* him! To be explicitly clear, God says in Isaiah 48:11, "For my own sake, for my own sake. . . . I will not yield my glory to another." God also says, "I am the LORD; that is my name! I will not give my glory to another or my praise to idols" (Isa. 42:8).

If God made us and gifted us to bring him glory, he must give us the means to pursue this worthy endeavor. Absolutely! Please notice the emphasis. Ecclesiastes 9:10 says, "*Whatever* your hand [or foot] finds to do, do it with all your might." (As a soccer coach, I added the word *foot* . . . but believe it is actually covered by the word *whatever.*) We see this again in 1 Corinthians 10:31: "So whether you eat or drink or *whatever* you do, do it all for the glory of God." Colossians 3:23–24 also emphasizes when and how we ought to bring God glory:

> *Whatever* you do, work at it with all your heart, as working for the Lord, not for men, since you know that you will receive an inheritance from the Lord as a reward. It is the Lord Christ you are serving.

18

As you pursue life and athletics in this manner, know that God will give you strength to accomplish the task he has given you to accomplish. Isaiah 40:29–31 says,

> He gives strength to the weary
>   and increases the power of the weak.
> Even youths grow tired and weary,
>   and young men stumble and fall;
> but those who hope in the LORD
>   will renew their strength.
> They will soar on wings like eagles;
>   they will run and not grow weary,
>   they will walk and not be faint.

There are times when we do not believe we have what it takes, and in our weakness, our hearts fail. However, in 2 Corinthians 12:9, Paul declares, "Therefore I will boast all the more gladly about my weaknesses, so that Christ's power may rest on me." Paul also notes where our confidence is derived:

> Such confidence as this is ours through Christ before God. Not that we are competent in ourselves to claim anything for ourselves, but our competence comes from God. (2 Cor. 3:4–5)

Paul also writes, "We are God's workmanship, created in Christ Jesus to do good works, which God *prepared in advance for us to do*" (Eph. 2:10). How freeing and empowering! Don't miss this point. This is where it all comes together. God made us, gifted us, and desires that we bring him glory in everything we do. He gives us the strength to do the good works he prepared for us before we were even born. Doesn't he see those good works through to completion? Absolutely!

So where do we come in? We are challenged to remain faithful using the talents and abilities God has entrusted to us.

Look at the parable of the talents, where the master responds to the servant who made good use of what he entrusted to him. "His master replied, 'Well done, good and faithful servant! You have been faithful with a few things; I will put you in charge of many things'" (Matt. 25:21).

There is one important caveat. When something goes well, we cannot take any credit for ourselves. Proverbs 21:31 says, "The horse is made ready for the day of battle, but victory rests with the LORD." Romans 11:36 adds, "From him and through him and to him are all things. To him be the glory forever!"

Writing to Timothy, Paul gives us a vision of what a life of faith looks like as it draws to a close. "I have fought the good fight," he tells Timothy, "I have finished the race, I have kept the faith" (2 Tim. 4:7). We are not promised a scoreboard win, which is why we must keep in mind Paul's reminder to live lives that are worthy of the gospel (Phil. 1:27).

For years people have looked to Eric Liddell as the example of how Christians can pursue athletics in the way I have described. Liddell was an extremely fast runner faced with several major life dilemmas. Because of race schedules, he had to choose to either run on Sunday and likely win but go against his personal convictions, or follow what he believed and forfeit running on the Sabbath. At the same time, his sister was strongly suggesting he go to China to be a missionary. While he knew mission work was worth pursuing, he was trying to reconcile the gift of running and speed God had given him. In *Chariots of Fire*, the movie based on his life, he explains why he runs: "I believe God made me for a purpose . . . but he also made me fast. And when I run I feel his pleasure."[1]

MODERN ATHLETES OF FAITH

But who thinks that way today? Who believes that faith affects all areas of our lives—even athletics? More people hold this perspective than you might imagine. Let me offer the examples of three men who live out this belief today: former Florida Gator and professional football quarterback Tim Tebow; Major League Baseball (MLB) player Josh Hamilton of the Texas Rangers; and Jeremy Lin from the National Basketball Association (NBA) Houston Rockets.

In his book, *Through My Eyes*, Tim Tebow notes, "I always thought since God gave these gifts to me, my role in that exchange was to play as hard as I could and continue to give Him the honor and glory for it. To me, that would be the very best way for thanking Him for the ability."[2] He continues, "To me, our Christian witness matters, and it's what people see when they are watching us. When we think we can do less than our best, when we think others are not watching, we're cheating ourselves and the God who created us."[3]

Josh Hamilton's story is about as different from Tebow's as possible. While Tebow is the "poster man" of a professional Christian athlete, Josh Hamilton has been led down a different path. He has squandered millions of dollars on drugs, gone in and out of drug rehab, been suspended from baseball, and been separated from his family. When he came to one of the lowest places in his life, he showed up at his grandmother's house at 2 a.m., weighing only 180 pounds and barely recognizable. He later described himself as "a wreck—dirty, twitchy and barely coherent."[4] However, he met Jesus and surrendered his life to Christ.

Hamilton did not become automatically perfect and still struggles with relapses. As a result of choices he has made, he is criticized and even taunted when he goes to the ballparks of rival teams. A 2012 *Sports Illustrated* cover story, "The Fragile Brilliance of Josh Hamilton," talks of how his faith has changed his response to reactions against him. Realizing that Jesus prayed for those who persecuted him, Hamilton began to look at the situation in a new light. The writer says, "That's why now if you watch him in the field, you'll sometimes see Hamilton's lips moving between pitches. He heard what you said. He's praying that you'll get better soon."[5]

In the book *Playing with Purpose* Hamilton notes that his dark, drug-riddled past has given him "a platform to share what [God has] done in [his] life." He goes on to say, "My wife was telling me that God was going to allow me to get back into baseball. It was going to be about sharing how He brought me through the storm."[6] Now known as one of the greatest players currently in baseball, Hamilton puts it in perspective when he says, "Baseball is third in my life right now, behind my relationship with God and my family. Without the first two, baseball isn't even in the picture. Believe me, I know."[7]

In May 2012, ESPN ran a story on Hamilton the day after he did what only sixteen players in all baseball have ever done—hit four homeruns in one game! It is interesting that the article begins this way: "He takes things one day at a time and lets his faith in Jesus Christ be a perpetual compass."[8] The world does not respond like this unless a person's faith is so visible that it compels them to pen such words. Josh Hamilton is a changed man with a love for his Jesus!

When asked about his big night, he replied, "I think about what God has done in my life, and everything I've done to mess it up. . . . What God has allowed me to do, to come back from everything I've been through and still be able to play the game at the level I play it—it's pretty amazing to think about that."[9]

Jeremy Lin's story is radically different from the stories of these two other men. He was never offered a basketball scholarship after high school. He was not drafted to the NBA after playing for Harvard University. In 2010, he was given a chance by the Golden State Warriors but was demoted to the

NBA D-League (development league) three times before being waived. The Houston Rockets picked him up, then quickly released him. Finally, on December 27, 2011, the New York Knicks picked him up.[10] The rest is history. Lin received a chance and never looked back. In one highlight, he scored 38 points in a win over the LA Lakers. Linsanity began![11]

However, this is not the best part of Lin's story. Lin has not bemoaned the fact that his journey to the NBA has been such a roller-coaster ride. In fact, he cites Romans 5:3–5, which reads:

> We also rejoice in our sufferings, because we know that suffering produces perseverance; perseverance, character; and character, hope. And hope does not disappoint us, because God has poured out his love into our hearts by the Holy Spirit, whom he has given us.

Lin understands that God is in control, working in the details of our lives. During an interview with a Taiwanese evangelical Christian channel, Lin said,

> The Bible talks a lot about how God takes bad situations and tough situations and he teaches us and he uses those times of suffering to draw us closer to him and that's what I try to focus on during those times. . . .
>
> There were just so many different things that really had to happen in order for me to make it into the NBA and you know I have a list of about 12 to 15 things that had to happen and none of it had anything to do with me and it was all in God's control. His fingerprints are all over my story.[12]

This perspective has impacted everything about Lin and how he pursues life and basketball. He said,

> To understand that I'm not playing for anything on this earth, I'm playing for my prize in heaven, for the upward call that

Paul talks about, that's what I need to remind myself every day when I wake up.

I [have] to really understand that I'm not playing for all my fans, for my family, even for myself, I really have to play to glorify God. . . . And when other people see me play basketball . . . the way I treat my teammates, the opponents, the refs, that's all a reflection of God's image and God's love so that's the stuff I try to focus on. . . .

Every time I step on the court and there are 20,000 fans screaming . . . I try to block everybody out and . . . just pretend like God is sitting courtside right there . . . and just play, play for him.[13]

What a perspective. He gets it. When asked how he can maintain this perspective, Lin replies that he understands he is a sinner saved by grace.[14]

While this is certainly not a guarantee in the Christian life, Lin's patience and perseverance was rewarded during the summer of 2012, when he was extended, and accepted, a three-year, $25.1 million contract with the Houston Rockets.

Three men with three different stories—one a well-known, deeply loved, and respected star athlete with a record of walking the straight and narrow, another with a story line of redemption and a new beginning, and yet another who rose from humble and modest beginnings to become, for a time, the most talked about name in basketball. Different men with different stories—yet binding them together is their love for Jesus Christ and their willingness to acknowledge him, follow him, and play for him. They have a drive to share their God with others and show what he has done for them as they live out their faith through athletics.

You may or may not compete on a grand scale like these men have in the NFL, MLB, or NBA. That is not the point. As your story continues and your season begins, what perspective will you hold about faith and athletics? How you answer this question changes everything! Clarity on this point will bring everything into focus, allowing you to use your giftedness and purposefully pursue athletics through your faith in Christ.

PERSONAL EVALUATION/DISCUSSION QUESTIONS

1. Prior to reading this chapter, what was your view of what it meant to be a Christian athlete? Has it changed? If yes, how so?

2. Which passages here did you identify with? Did they cause you to view faith and athletics from a perspective that you previously had not held? Share the verse and explain the change in perspective.

3. Do you disagree with anything about the perspective that is described in this chapter? Explain.

4. In your own words, summarize what it means for your faith and athletics to merge.

5. Of the three examples of Christian professional athletes, whose story do you identify with the most? How so? How is their story encouraging to you?

STAGE 1

PRESEASON

"The credit belongs to the man . . . who spends himself for a worthy cause . . . so that his place shall never be with those cold and timid souls who knew neither victory nor defeat."[1]

—*Theodore Roosevelt*

"Do not let what you cannot do interfere with what you can do."[2]

—*John Wooden*

> Therefore, my beloved brothers, be steadfast, immovable, always abounding in the work of the Lord, knowing that in the Lord your labor is not in vain. (1 Cor. 15:58 ESV)
>
> —*Jacob Warren, #5, defender*

CHAPTER TWO

RISK YOUR BEST

*"I will not sacrifice to the LORD my God
burnt offerings that cost me nothing."*
—*2 Samuel 24:24*

HEADLINES

- Preseason provides a new beginning.
- Offering your best can be risky. . . . Do it anyway.
- Risk involves responsibility, exceeding expectations, and refusing to compromise.
- Taking such risks will leave you with no regrets.

CONSIDER THIS BOLD STATEMENT made by former U.S. soccer forward Mia Hamm: "Many people say that I am the best soccer player in the world. I don't think so. And because of that, someday I just might be."[1] Before the start of her sophomore season, Hamm sat down for a meeting with her University of North Carolina soccer coach, Anson Dorrance, who also happened to be the coach of the U.S. National Women's Team. He asked her what her goals were for the upcoming season. She replied, "To be the best." Looking back, Hamm said,

Saying you want to be at the very top of your field and doing it are two different things. Saying it is exhilarating and a little scary because you are making a choice to stand out from the crowd; doing it is incredibly hard work. You can't ever live with 'good enough'. Sometimes, deciding to be the best feels great. Sometimes it's discouraging, and almost always it's exhausting. The bottom line is, if I don't go into it every day consistently committed, I won't get results.[2]

When Hamm made that risky commitment to be the best, she meant it. At age fifteen she was already playing for the U.S. National Team. At nineteen, she was the youngest team member to win the World Cup in 1991. She was elected Soccer USA's Female Athlete of the Year five years in a row (1994–98), was Most Valued Player (MVP) of the Women's Cup in 1995, and won three Excellence in Sports Performance Yearly awards, including Soccer Player of the Year and Female Athlete of the Year. In 2004, she and teammate Michelle Akers joined FIFA's list of the 125 greatest living soccer players, the only two women and only two Americans to be named. She continues to hold the record for the most international goals scored (158), male or female.[3]

However, her focus on individual success was for the betterment of her teams. In college she helped to guide the North Carolina women's soccer team to four consecutive National College Athletic Association championships. She helped her team to win the gold in the summer Olympics in 1996 and 2004 and again led the U.S. National Team to a World Cup gold medal in 1999. When Mia Hamm said that she wanted to be the best, she opened herself up for disappointment and scrutiny, yet she clearly accomplished her goal.[4]

A NEW BEGINNING

One of my absolute favorite times of the year comes when preseason training rolls around. There is excitement in the air because players are fresh, eager, and filled with hope for what the new season will bring them as individuals and the team as a whole. Some want to build on the success of the previous season or establish themselves as team leaders. Others simply want to make the team.

Regardless of the perspectives players bring to opening day, each one must be willing to risk his or her best. This may sound odd, yet the reality is that many players struggle to do this, particularly during preseason training. Some hold back from risking or offering their best because in the backs of their minds they are concerned about failure.

Athletes often come across as confident men and women who have it all together. In reality, many athletes are more insecure than they care to admit. When a situation looks like a guaranteed victory, they go hard and invest deeply because they believe they will come out on top. These types of players are often referred to as ego-oriented players. They want to know that the situation will turn out well for them because they have a reputation and status to protect. However, ego-oriented players feel unsettled and tentative about pursuing risks when the outcome does not appear certain.

Players who are going out for the team for the first time experience many of these same fears. For different reasons, these players are all concerned that if they offer their best, it may not be good enough. This can have paralyzing effects on such players and be a major hindrance for the team's developmental success. For any team to be successful, a culture must be developed where players are willing to make "risky" investments. For that reason, it's important that coaches provide encouraging environments where there is freedom to fail—with the big-picture perspective that the team culture can pay off over the course of a season.

While it's the coach's responsibility to set the tone and develop team culture, players can do much to contribute to these dynamics even before preseason begins. Below are four ways in which you as a player can assist in shaping successful team culture. To do this, though, you will need to risk your best.

Offer Your Best!

Over the last decade, NBA players such as Kobe Bryant, Dwayne Wade, and LeBron James have been compared to Michael Jordan. After the Miami Heat lost to the Dallas Mavericks in the 2011 NBA championship, I was listening to ESPN radio. The talk show host berated LeBron James, saying his name should never be put in the same sentence as Michael Jordan's again. He actually said that if that topic were to come up, he would go silent on the air and refuse to talk about the comparison.

While Jordan's NBA championship rings, scoring titles, and MVP trophies are certainly worthy of high recognition, it is worth noting what propelled him to such greatness. Obviously Jordan was blessed with incredible athleticism. What separated him from the contenders, however, was a competitiveness that drove him to train and prepare in a way unparalleled by his competition. This drive also motivated his teammates. Jordan had what he called the "breakfast club": his own personal training that he did in his gym early in the morning before his coach called practice. It didn't take long for his supporting cast to join him.

Michael Jordan was extremely serious about training and preparing. He viewed training as an area of his life that he could control, and he mastered it. The results spoke for themselves. He not only helped his team to win six NBA championships, but he could be counted on to come through in each and every match. Consequently he was named MVP for each of those NBA championships. In addition, Jordan was the league's MVP five times, was a three-time All-Star MVP, was named to the all-star team fourteen times, and at the end of the 1987–88 season was named the Defensive Player of the Year, with over 200 blocked shots and over 100 steals.[5] He had trained and prepared to offer his best at both ends of the court.

Raise the Bar

Most coaches give players a preseason training regimen to complete before they come to the first day of training. The coach's requirements must be the minimum standard for players to meet. As a college soccer player, I was not the most skilled player on the team. However, I knew I could be the fittest and most well-conditioned player. That was in my control, and I pursued it vigorously! After struggling my sophomore year, I took my coach's summer training program and simply doubled what he asked of us. On days that we had a five-mile run, I ran ten. When we were required to do speed and agility work, I doubled the number and did it at top speed in the heat of the day. When the first day of training camp finally came, I found great satisfaction in accomplishing what I had set out to achieve.

Unfortunately, too many players look at these training regimens as optional. In college it was easy to pick out the guys who did not do the training program. They would try to hang with the players who had, but they inevitably pulled a muscle or got injured within the first several days of training. They had not prepared their muscles for the rigor their bodies were suddenly trying to sustain.

Over the years I have found that there is often a direct correlation between the number of players who complete preseason training programs and the number of very successful players. Yet there is not always a correlation between a player's talent level and his or her work ethic. Often the most talented players are not the hardest workers. Players like Hamm and Jordan were the best in their respective sports. When their careers ended, people knew they had witnessed something incredibly special. Much of this had to do with the time they dedicated to training off the field or court. They expected their teammates to train and prepare in the same way. They had a tireless work ethic, a willingness to invest their best in everything they did . . . and that attitude became contagious to those around them.

This is not always the case with superstar athletes, such as NBA player Allen Iverson. Iverson won individual scoring titles, but he doesn't have one NBA championship ring to wear. One of his career-defining moments came in a news conference when he admitted to being flabbergasted that he was being held accountable for missing a practice and could not see how this would hurt his teammates. His career in the NBA came to an end without fanfare or special recognition.

Team sports ultimately recognize the success of the team, not individual achievements. This is why great players are deeply disappointed with a team loss even though they themselves may have played an exceptional game. Truly great players value team success over their own individual success. Top players must regularly ask themselves how their actions affect those around them. Are they inspiring others to meet their potential and excel? Or are they causing their teammates to have a "get by" attitude?

One of my favorite lines comes from the movie *Miracle*, the true story of the 1976 U.S. Olympic Hockey team. This team, made up only of college hockey players, accomplished the unimaginable when it defeated the machine-like Soviet Union team to win the gold medal. The line I love is "The legs feed the wolf."[6] When you are fit, you can do what the coach asks of you. Without the training and the willingness to invest, you will not be able to achieve success no matter how badly you want it.

Do Not Compromise

Once you begin your training, whether you are doing the minimum your coach expects or a more rigorous program that you have established for yourself, you must be disciplined and allow for no compromises. When pressed due to scheduling conflicts, fatigue, soreness, or any other excuse, you can quickly convince yourself that it won't hurt to take off a day. One day can quickly become two or three days, and then suddenly you have abandoned the program. Set your sights on what you want to accomplish and don't back down.

The late Chicago Bears running back Walter Payton noted, "The only way you can perform is to prepare and condition yourself."[7] He told an ESPN reporter that he had found a hill near his home that was eighty yards long at a 45-degree angle. He gathered some of his teammates to train together on this hill. The first time they tried to run the hill, they could only do it twice. However, by the time they reported to training camp, he and the other players could run it twenty-five times consecutively. He went to the Pro Bowl nine times, was the NFL's Player of the Year in 1977 and 1985, and was elected into the Hall of Fame in 1993. His former teammate, defensive end Richard Dent, told the *Chicago Tribune*, "He's been a great person to me in teaching you how to be the best at anything. He worked twice as hard as we did."[8] Payton knew that staying on top requires extra work to be successful.

One of the top five soccer players who ever played for me stood 5'3" short as a freshman. Yet Matt Smith was determined to make the team. Although he had exceptional skill, I wondered if he could survive the physicality of the competitions we played. He set out to prove that he could. Throughout the summer he exceeded the training program I had given the players. He tirelessly trained six days a week while wearing a twenty-pound vest. I would drive by the soccer field and see him on his own doing ball work and sprints. His practices were so intense that he would go to the side of the field, throw up, and get right back to his training regimen. Few high school players, let alone a rising ninth grader, ever push themselves to that degree.

Matt made the team his freshman year and even earned a starting position. However, he was not satisfied. He had greater aspirations and refused to relent. His training program prior to ninth grade became his summer training program for the next three years. He concluded his four years of high school with two state championship titles, scoring the game-winning goals in each of the matches. He also earned a state runner-up title, having lost to the team of DaMarcus Beasley, a U.S. National Team player. He was named first team All-State for three years and broke the school's goal-scoring record with 110 goals. By his sophomore year in college, he was an All-American. Matt refused to compromise. He would not back down from my expectations and the even higher bar that he set for himself. The outcome speaks for itself.

Have No Regrets

While there may never again be another Michael Jordan, there could be more Matt Smiths out there if they would simply risk their best. Instead, these young men and women may hold back out of fear of failure or because they don't believe they have what it takes. They convince themselves that they have offered their best effort or that the work is too hard. They refuse to press through temporary discomfort.

Little I can say will get you to do what I am proposing, for your drive to work hard must come from within. However, I can assure you that if you dedicate yourself to doing your absolute best and, with a clear heart and mind, know that you could not have done more, regardless of outcome, you will be at peace. Knowing that you offered your best, you will be able to hold your head high and accept the verdict. While others may criticize and critique and compare, if you have risked your best, you will have no regrets. In a speech called "Citizenship in a Republic," President Theodore Roosevelt said,

> It is not the critic who counts: not the man who points out how the strong man stumbles or where the doer of deeds could have done better. The credit belongs to the man who is actually in the arena, whose face is marred by dust and sweat and blood, who strives valiantly, who errs and comes up short again and again, because there is no effort without error or shortcoming, but who knows the great enthusiasms, the great devotions, who spends himself for a worthy cause; who, at the best, knows, in the end, the triumph of high achievement, and who, at the worst, if he fails, at least he fails while daring greatly, so that his place shall never be with those cold and timid souls who knew neither victory nor defeat.[9]

AGAINST ALL ODDS

In 1995 I started a girls' soccer team at the high school where I was teaching. This was a difficult endeavor. Plenty of naysayers were not interested in adding girls' soccer to our athletic program, particularly because it would coincide with the girls' basketball season. Although the boys' soccer team had won the state championship and a state runner-up title in the previous two years, many thought girls' soccer would not survive and that it was foolish to try. In fact, during preseason, teachers told some of the girls that the team shouldn't exist and probably would not win one single game.

We knew risks and challenges lay ahead of us but instead of allowing them to serve as a source of discouragement, we used them as motivation to work just a bit harder. Since most of our girls were in eighth or ninth grade, we played a partial junior varsity and varsity schedule during the inaugural season. We finished that season 14–0–1. In the second year we played an all-varsity schedule and finished with a winning record and a district championship. By the third season we were one game away from the state tournament and lost to the eventual state champs, finishing with a 21–3–1 record. We had almost every reason at every turn not to add the team. Despite the odds, we stayed true and unswerving to our course, and I am proud to say that girls' soccer is a strong and vibrant program today!

Throughout your life, you will be challenged in unusual ways. Know that sometimes even those who call you "friend" will wish for your downfall. In my early years of coaching, I heard a coach say that one should never listen to too much praise or too much criticism. That advice has served me well over the years, because I have received plenty of both. If you are not careful, both will distract you and cause you to back away from offering your best. Keeping a steady, focused, and balanced perspective on successes and failures allows you to focus on the process or steps along the journey. The challenge is to be steady, stay the course, and give your best effort regardless of short-term victories or setbacks.

PERSONAL EVALUATION/DISCUSSION QUESTIONS

1. When have you held back from risking your best? What reasons can you identify for not investing wholeheartedly?

2. If you have compromised in your preparation, recall when the compromise began. What steps will you need to take to ensure you do not compromise this season?

3. Few athletes are as self-determined and driven as those I mentioned in this chapter. Even the greats choose to train together. Who might serve with you as a training partner and provide accountability to help you to stay the course? What needs to take place to make this partner training happen?

4. What might you accomplish this season (in life) if you train and prepare in a manner where you will have no regrets? What if your team trains and prepares in this way? What realistic outcomes might your team accomplish?

5. Go back and ask these questions again as you reflect on your life outside athletics. Consider three personal issues you are processing even now, e.g., relationships, school, work, etc.

This day I call heaven and earth as witnesses against you that I have set before you life and death, blessings and curses. Now choose life, so that you and your children may live and that you may love the LORD your God, listen to his voice, and hold fast to him. For the LORD is your life, and he will give you many years in the land he swore to give to your fathers, Abraham, Isaac and Jacob. (Deut. 30:19–20)

— *Tim Love, #16, center midfielder*

CHAPTER THREE

SELECTED

"But select capable men from all the people."
—Exodus 18:21

HEADLINES

- Being selected to a team roster is a privilege.
- Individual player assimilation to the team is vital.
- Players should know *why* they are selected to a team.
- When called on to fill a greater role, be sure to be prepared.
- Egos and personal agenda delay or prevent forward progress.

ARNOLD JACOB "RED" AUERBACH, the late coach and president of the Boston Celtics, said it well: "How you select people is more important than how you manage them once they're on your team. If you start with the right people, you won't have problems later on."[1]

NUMBER 199

Despite a fairly successful career at the University of Michigan, Tom Brady was not hoping for the 2000 NFL draft. Scouts cast him in a less than favorable light, with one report noting, "Poor build, very skinny and narrow, lacks mobility and the ability to avoid the rush, lacks a really strong arm."[2] These are not the words you want attached to your name when you are looking for an NFL team to notice you, select you, and make an investment in you.

After he had watched six quarterbacks get selected before him in six draft rounds, the New England Patriots finally selected him at number 199. The Patriots already had three quarterbacks. Why had they chosen a player like Tom Brady? He hadn't even won the full-time starting position until his senior year at Michigan. However, the coaching staff must have seen something in Brady that caused them to draft him.

The rest is history. The chance the Patriots took on Brady paid off more than they could have dreamed as he led them to three Super Bowl championships. In 2005, Brady won the highly coveted *Sports Illustrated* Sportsman of the Year award and has won two Super Bowl MVP awards, been elected to seven Pro Bowls, and holds the NFL record for the most touchdown passes in a single regular season. He was named the 2007 and 2010 NFL MVP as well as 2007 Male Athlete of the Year.[3]

YOU EARNED IT!

Even more exciting than the first day of preseason training is when the team roster is announced for the new season. Not only do the players who make the team feel a great sense of relief and accomplishment, but as a coach, I cannot wait to begin investing in a group of players who will be spending a great deal of time together. As a player, it is vital for you to understand what it means to be on the team roster.

Very few coaches offer courtesy spots on a team. Being selected to a team is quite an accomplishment. The older you get and the higher the level of play becomes, the more difficult it is to make the team due to greater competition. Each year I closely watch the new players. Beyond their obvious playing ability, I am interested in their work ethic and how they get along with other players. I also look for those subtleties in a player's life that demonstrate how he or she will respond to my coaching philosophy and the rest of the players. I watch for

- how players handle themselves off the field when they think no one is looking,
- how they respond when another player offers advice or even correction during tryouts,
- how they do the little things, such as finish a sprint or go for a ball that is going out of bounds,
- what their body language communicates when their team is losing or up by a lot,
- what they do during the time between their arrival and the time that I bring the players into the huddle to speak with them,
- and if they pay attention and focus when I or other coaches are speaking.

When the time comes for making player selection, I use a chart that outlines the most important qualities that we are looking for in a player. To avoid making hasty, one-sided decisions, I have found it very helpful to have my assistant coaches and even captains rate the new players as well. We compile and analyze the results for each player who has tried out for the team. We consider how each player would best complement the players currently in our system and aid us in what we are trying to accomplish as a program. While I have the final say as head coach, the input from my assistant coaches and the captains is invaluable! There have been times when they have convinced me either to keep or not keep a player . . . and for good reasons.

I say this so that you might understand that when coaches watch you, typically more is going on than meets the eye. As the competition becomes stiffer and a program becomes more successful, the criteria to make the team become focused, deliberate, and intense. You may recall a time when you saw a player selected to a team and were surprised by that selection. It's important for you as a player to know what your coach is looking for on the front end.

You should also know that while your coach may give you a list of important characteristics for selection, some intangibles will never show up on a player review or scouting card. Most coaches are very concerned, and rightfully so, about team dynamics and cohesiveness. Red Auerbach said, "Some people believe you will win with the five best players, but I found out that you will win with the five who fit together best."[4]

Now that you have a glimpse of the scrutiny you have undergone, you should be struck by the fact that you earned a position on the team. You have a specific role and task that you must press toward with all the vigor and passion you can muster. I will say more about this in later chapters.

SELECTED FOR A REASON

A whole book in the Bible is dedicated to the story of redemption involving a young Jewish girl. Through a series of providential events, Esther becomes the queen of Persia. When a scheming and jealous man called Haman makes a plot to kill all the Jews, Esther's uncle Mordecai tells her that God caused her to become queen "for such a time as this" (Esther 4:14). In other words, it was no accident that she, a Jewish girl, was chosen to be queen. If she had ever wondered why such an amazing thing had happened to her, the answer may have become clear as her uncle pleaded with her to use her access to the king to save her people.

Players are selected by a coach to be on the team roster for a specific purpose or "for such a time as this." When a coach selects you, it's important for you to know that he or she believes in you and sees that you can fill a specific role. Your job is to do everything in your power to fulfill that role. Never be satisfied just to be on the team. If you are unsure of your role, ask your coach about his or her vision for how you can best contribute to the success of the team. This is important for you to know and for your coach to share with you. In order to train and prepare with purpose, you must have something to strive toward. Once you know what to do, get after it.

Our 2011 soccer team was twenty-one players deep. When the second group came on the field, they understood their mission and how it factored into the overall success of the team. Their job was to hound the opposition and to wear it down before the starters came back into the match. They began to take great pride in their role. When they saw the success the starters had when they reentered the game as the opposition was fading, the players in the second group knew they had been successful in their role.

DON'T SETTLE—BE READY FOR YOUR CHANCE

Although Tom Brady was drafted by the New England Patriots, he had no guarantee that he would even make the team. However, he ended up playing well in preseason and training camp and won the third quarterback roster spot. Despite only one game appearance and one completed pass as a rookie, he was not discouraged. He continued to work extremely hard and prepare for the moment when he would be called to step in the game.

In his second season with the Patriots (2001), Brady moved up the depth chart and became the direct backup to starting quarterback Drew Bledsoe. Just two weeks into the season, Bledsoe was hurt in a game against the New York Jets. This was Brady's moment! He entered the game and completed five passes for forty-six yards. The next week, Brady started his first NFL game versus the Indianapolis Colts.[5] He started the rest of the regular thirteen season games, and the Patriots finished the season with an 11–5 record, an American Football Conference (AFC) East division title, and a playoff berth. That year he threw for 2,843 yards, had eighteen touchdowns, and made the AFC Pro Bowl team![6] Brady knew that he could not waste any chance he was given because the opportunity might not come around again.

For you to be ready for that moment, you must have a healthy sense of discontentment. While your coach might have designated a role for you to play, be prepared for a greater role. The day might come when you are asked to fill a new role for the greater good of the team. Be ready for that moment. If you are asked to step up, you don't want to be physically unfit, mentally unprepared, and tactically clueless about what the team has been doing and how you should execute what is being asked of you.

John Wooden said, "If you don't have time to do it right, when will you have time to do it over?"[7] He was right on the mark. As I noted in chapter one, Jeremy Lin is a perfect example of this. He worked hard, refused to give up, and, when given the opportunity, he took hold of it and was prepared to do it right!

I will never forget when a young man by the name of Zach Hall stepped onto the field during our 2007 district championship match. With four minutes remaining in regulation, we had scored to tie the game 1–1. We then played two ten-minute periods of overtime and began the sudden death periods. The other team had a very fast outside midfielder. Zach had good speed and big heart. I subbed him into the game to mark this player and prevent him from scoring on us.

With minutes remaining on the clock in the second period of sudden death, a ball came across the mouth of the goal.

Suddenly Zach came out of nowhere to slam the ball into the back of the net for the victory. Our players poured onto the field and hoisted Zach onto their shoulders. As the dust settled, everything made sense. Although none of us could have predicted that moment, Zach had prepared for it. He had often stayed after practice to run extra sprints and do additional speed and quickness training. All those sprints and extra hours of training had come down to that one moment. When asked about it, he is quick to say that it was all worth it!

DROP THE EGO AND PERSONAL AGENDAS

While you should have a healthy spirit of discontentment to propel you to work harder on behalf of your team, you should also check your ego at the door. Nothing is more destructive to a team than for an individual to elevate himself or herself above the team or the coach's decisions. While individual goals are fine, they must always be subordinate to the coach's vision for the team and the team's larger goals.

In my second year of coaching, the two highest scoring players began to notice their individual goal count and compare themselves to each other. It came to a head during one of our last regular season games. One of those players came over to me on the sideline during the match and asked me to substitute the other leading scorer. He asked because the player had just scored, and with one more goal he would pass him in total number of goals scored for the season. I'm sure most can guess which player came off the field at the next available substitution!

When your focus begins to turn inward, remember that you earned a spot on your team for a specific reason and purpose. Staying focused on that purpose, with a team spirit, will keep you in check as you progress through the season.

These same principles apply when you are looking for summer employment or going through the college admission process. In both cases, you have to earn the position and prove that you are a worthy candidate. The old adage that there is "no free lunch" is almost always true. Employers or college admissions directors will come to a point where they need to make a decision about whether or not they will select you. You'll want to have prepared yourself to be in the best position possible so you'll have no regrets. All too often, students come into my office almost in tears. As juniors, they realize they have wasted their first two years of high school and probably won't get into the university of their choice.

As noted in the first chapter, the parable of the talents (Matt. 25:14–30) illustrates this brilliantly. In this story, the master goes on a journey and gives his three servants coins to invest during his absence. When he returns, he investigates how each servant has managed his money. Two of the servants were faithful with what he had entrusted to them; they had invested the money, causing the amount to double. The third servant had buried the money in the ground and done nothing with what the master had entrusted to him. Hearing this, the master calls the third servant wicked and lazy (v. 26), then orders the money to be taken from him because he had squandered what had been graciously given to him. To each of the two servants who invested wisely, the master says, "Well done, good and faithful servant! You have been faithful with a few things; I will put you in charge of many things. Come and share your master's happiness!" (vv. 21, 23).

When you are given an opportunity in athletics, employment, education, or anything else, do the most with what you have. Female Basketball great Lisa Leslie understood what it meant to be given an opportunity and not take it for granted. In 1994 the Brazilians stunned the US team at the 1994 world championships. As a player on that team, Leslie recalls the pain she experienced. She vowed, "I will never put this uniform on again and experience losing." And she never did.

The 6'5" center led Team USA to Olympic gold in 1996, 2000, 2004, and 2008, as well as to world championships in 1998 and 2002. In reflection, she said, "I always felt like the biggest honor was to represent our country. The desire to not lose was so strong, almost stronger than the desire to win, if that makes sense."[8]

Act from the wellspring of your heart for the advancement of the team, company, or institution as instructed by the one in charge. You will not regret such a decision.

PERSONAL EVALUATION/DISCUSSION QUESTIONS

1. What is your role on the team? If you don't know your role, what must you do to find it out?

2. How would you describe your level of commitment to the specific role your coach has for you?

3. Consider the current role you play. What is the next level of responsibility that requires more effort, dedication, and commitment? What are the first steps that you need to take to be ready to fill that role? Are you ready to begin those steps? When will you begin?

4. As you consider life outside athletics, ask yourself these same questions. Although I ask these questions with athletics in mind, they can apply to all areas of your life. Some possibilities are academics, spiritual or devotional life, relationships with friends, job performance, or (fill in the blank). Ask yourself these questions and then take deliberate steps to be prepared to progress to the next level of excellence in the specific area you have identified.

Do not be deceived: "Bad company ruins good morals."
(1 Cor. 15:33 ESV)

—*Beau Simmons, #19, forward*

CHAPTER FOUR

THE RULES OF ENGAGEMENT

"So we rebuilt the wall till all of it reached half its
height, for the people worked with all their heart."
—*Nehemiah 4:6*

HEADLINES

- Collective agreement to abide by your team's rules of engagement is a must.
- Own and embrace the rules of engagement; don't merely comply.
- Though sometimes subtle, dissention can be deadly to a team.
- Positive leadership from within can solidify a team's direction and potential.

THE DESCENT OF GREATNESS

Every year professional or collegiate athletes make the headlines for violating team rules or even a general code of conduct. With these violations comes public attention and scrutiny. Few have received more attention in the past decade than the story of football great Michael Vick.

Michael was born in Newport News, Virginia; an area dominated by drugs and gang activity.[1] However, his big ticket "out" was football. As an extremely gifted athlete he caught the attention of college recruiters around the nation. He elected to stay close to home and attend Virginia Tech. During his first full season with the Hokies, he led them to an undefeated season before they fell to Florida State in the national title game. He was named the Big East's Offensive Player of the Year and finished third in the Heisman Trophy voting.[2]

Vick passed up his last two years of college to play in the NFL. He was selected as the #1 player in the 2001 NFL draft and was rewarded with a six-year, $62 million contract that included a $15 million signing bonus. By 2004, Vick had become a prolific franchise quarterback and was soon offered a massive 10-year, $130 million contract extension.[3]

Vick had become what many young athletes can only dream of becoming. However, in April 2007, authorities raided his Virginia property as they uncovered a private side of Vick that had been kept from the public eye. Soon the world knew that Vick was involved in a vicious dog-fighting ring that included the abuse and even killing of dogs. After a thorough investigation and a five-hour grilling by FBI agents, Vick admitted to killing dogs himself. "I did it all," he is reported to have said. "I did everything. If you need me to say more, I'll say more."[4]

In his book *Finally Free* (released 2012), Vick recalls a less than favorable memory when he notes, "It was a very nervous time for me. I knew I was going to try to lie my way through the whole dogfighting case and see if money, good lawyers, and manipulating the system could get me out of the position I was in—which was a terrible position."[5]

It was not long before it all caught up to him, as he was soon released by the Atlanta Falcons, banned from playing in the NFL, and sentenced to twenty-three months in prison. Choices made by Michael Vick had devastating results on both his personal and his professional life. In *Finally Free* he said, "I was no longer No. 7, the football player. I was inmate No. 33765-183, and I couldn't change that, regardless of the fact that this number definitely didn't fit me. I had that number on every day. I had to write it on each piece of mail that I sent out. It will forever be embedded in my brain."[6]

Thankfully, this is not the end of the story for Michael Vick. His story moves from rags to riches to prison and now redemption. In a statement issued after being released from prison, he said,

> I take full responsibility for my actions. . . . Not for one second will I sit right here and point the finger and try to blame anybody else for my actions or what I've done. . . . I'm upset with myself, and, you know, through this situation I found Jesus and asked him for forgiveness and turned my life over to God.[7]

> Pre-incarceration, it was all about me. When I got to prison, I realized I couldn't do it anymore. The one thing I could rely on was my faith in God. . . . Five months ago I was worried with what was going to happen, but now I'm more at peace. God has taken it over. I don't have to worry about being dynamic. God is in control of that.[8]

Michael Vick is back in the NFL, playing football for the Philadelphia Eagles. It is interesting to see the transformation of a man. Early in his career, much of his life was about what he wanted and not considering the cost to his teammates, the coaches, and the organization that drafted him. During October–November 2012 Vick had been knocked out of games with multiple concussions. As a result, certain people, even his own brother, have been openly critical of his offensive line for not protecting him better. However, he has learned from his past. He has been very quick to defend his linemen as he has been vocal about his appreciation, support and love for his teammates and their effort.[9]

While he now has a great redemption story, Vick would love to take back and change many things. Might this serve as a valuable lesson for what it means when one is selected and then commits to a team.

Every individual team must have team rules and guidelines that are followed and supported both publicly and privately. Players who break the rules rarely consider the outcome of their actions. Sometimes it never even occurs to them that they might be caught!

DECISION TIME

It's exciting when players are selected by the coach. We all desire to be noticed, wanted, and known. However, players have an opportunity to decline the offer to be a member of a specific team. This might almost sound absurd, but it makes perfect sense. Consider this in the context of an employee-to-employer relationship. When a potential employee (player) is offered a job, he or she is extended an invitation to join that company (team). However, the job offer is accompanied by the terms of the contract or a letter of agreement that specifies the expectations for the employee in what is typically referred to as the "code of conduct."

Contracts are extended with the understanding that the employee will embrace or uphold the rules that guide and direct the company's culture and ethos. When potential employees turn down a contract, it is often because the terms of the agreement are not to their liking.

The same is true for college admittance. Every year, I see high school seniors weighing the pros and cons of different colleges they might attend. Most seniors have applied to multiple colleges and are considering where they will spend the next four years of their lives. Many factor a college's code of conduct into their decision.

With this perspective, it's reasonable to link the player's acceptance of a spot on the team roster with his or her agreement to support the team's philosophy, points of emphasis, and team guidelines. These are designed for healthy and orderly team dynamics and culture.

If you feel you cannot support the team's "rules of engagement" as a player or are not willing to address and work through whatever the issues of conflict may be, it is only fair that you not try out for the team. Not only will you potentially take someone else's spot on the team, but you will set yourself on a crash course for serious conflict. This does not mean that you cannot disagree or hold a different opinion. In fact, over the course of the year, conflicts and disagreements are bound to occur, and as we will see, they can even be healthy for a team's growth and development. However, proper procedures should be in place for dealing with these matters.

PLAYER, PARENT, COACH COVENANT

Another tool I have used for years is what I refer to as a *parent, player, and coach covenant.* It is intended to identify roles and expectations while guiding players on how to address the inevitable challenges of either disagreement or conflict that might arise. Below are a few of the key points of the covenant that acts as our "rules of engagement" to live by.

- Playing for Chattanooga Christian School's Men's Soccer is a privilege and not a right.
- Violation of team rules of engagement will likely mean loss of playing time or potential removal from the team.
- I am a student first and an athlete second, and my priorities must be in accord.

- I am an individual who must submit to and support the overall "team first" philosophy in regard to field positions, playing time, personal glorification, team tactics, and overall coaching decisions.
- I must first pray about any concern I may have regarding coaching decisions. If the issue is still a major concern for me after seeking the Lord's will, I will set up a meeting with the coach. (We ask that parents follow the same guidelines. We also encourage parents to allow their sons to address concerns with the coaches first and see if there is a proper resolution.)
- If I choose to smoke, drink alcohol, or do drugs, I recognize I have chosen to be suspended from school and the team.
- My role may change from game to game or at various points of the season. My playing time may increase or decrease depending on individual ability and its relationship to the team's tactical perspective implemented by the coaches.
- The team always takes precedence over my individual personal likes, dislikes, preferences, and personal opinions (i.e., team dress, eating habits, being punctual, dates, etc.).
- The parents' roles are to support their sons and the coaches, to model Christ-like behavior during matches, and to give their sons encouragement and wise biblical counsel on how to handle dilemmas and controversies that may arise over the course of the season.
- I understand and agree to the terms mentioned above. I recognize I will reap the benefits or consequences based on my response to this covenant.

Each player and parent, along with the head coach, signs this document so all parties are on the same page. This partial list is for my own team, but each coach has his or her own rules that govern how the team will best function. I understand that it seems very formal, but it is better to have team guidelines laid out, discussed, and agreed on prior to the season. I have had to refer back to this covenant with players and with parents. I keep a copy in my coaching notebook at all times to remind myself what I have agreed to uphold and support as a coach. These terms are for my team—what about yours? What guides and directs your team?

OWN IT

As you consider the rules of engagement for your team and wrestle with your personal position and response, I challenge you to move from simple compliance at an intellectual level to embrace the team's terms at a deeper heart level. If you falter at this point or brush these rules aside, you can almost count on conflict in the future. The conflict may manifest itself in an external form of frustration and confusion or may simmer in the unrest of your own heart. Often discontentedness begins in the quietness of your own heart. If no peace or resolution is made, that discontentedness can have adverse affects on the team.

Proverbs 4:23 says, "Above all else, *guard* your heart, for it is the wellspring of life." Jesus adds clarity to this statement when he says, "The good man brings good things out of the good stored up in his heart, and the evil man brings evil things out of the evil stored up in his heart. For out of the overflow of his heart his mouth speaks" (Luke 6:45). When the pressure is on, when things are not going as planned, when disagreement with decisions begins to take root, it is certainly a time for you to be cautious and guard your heart. Otherwise what is in there almost certainly will spill over and out, and it is typically not good.

In fact, we often begin to think things of others that are not true at all. If a coach has not been giving you the playing time you believe you deserve, you may find that you are growing bitter toward your coach. If you have had no conversations with him or her about your concern, you might convince yourself that the coach does not like you and has some personal problem with you as a player. Things can quickly go from bad to worse when you vocalize your frustrations to someone other than your coach. You can always find someone who sides with your position! In fact, be aware that when we disagree with someone, our natural inclination is to find someone who will side with us. At this point, bitterness might grow to a cancerous level that destroys the team.

Unfortunately, the higher the stakes, the greater the cost and the most potential for team fractures and division. The book of James provides a wonderful gut-check for a person struggling to control his or her tongue. James writes, "The tongue also is a fire, a world of evil among the parts of the body. It corrupts the whole person, sets the whole course of his life on fire" (James 3:6) and continues, "It is a restless evil, full of deadly poison" (v. 8). Later James says, "Where you have envy and selfish ambition, there you find disorder and every evil practice" (v. 16). I bet you're getting the point!

FIND COMMON GROUND

In the movie *Remember the Titans*, Coach Boone recognizes that he has major problems on his football team. Setting off to preseason team camp, he establishes his "rules of engagement" before any player even gets on the bus. However, he quickly realizes that there is major racial division among the players, and his own coaching staff is conflicted about who should lead the team. Frustration runs high as tensions mount.

When Boone gets his team up at 3 a.m. the next day, he has something much bigger and grander planned than just a long run. His mission that morning has little to do with physical training and everything to do with heart training. He wakes up his players to take them to a specific place for a specific purpose. Their destination is Gettysburg. Standing on the field, he delivers the following words to a physically exhausted and relationally divided group of young men:

> This is where they fought the battle of Gettysburg. Fifty thousand men died right here on this field, fighting the same fight that we are still fighting among ourselves today. This green field right here, painted red, bubblin' with the blood of young boys. Smoke and hot lead pouring right through their bodies. Listen to their souls, men. "I killed my brother with malice in my heart. Hatred destroyed my family." You listen, and you take a lesson from the dead. If we don't come together right now on this hallowed ground, we too will be destroyed, just like they were. I don't care if you like each other or not, but you will respect each other. And maybe . . . I don't know, maybe we'll learn to play this game like men.[10]

Boone recognized that it did not matter how much football they talked about, how many sessions a day they ran during preseason training, or what type of talent they had on the team. It came down to their relationships with each other. Even the coaches didn't respect and believe in each other. If they were going to have any success during the season, Boone knew it was imperative for them to embrace each other as brothers but also to embrace the team's ground rules.

OWNERSHIP AND BUY-IN

A team covenant supported by the entire team (coaches, players, and parents) provides a tool for a great deal of self-regulation and can help the team to move forward in a healthy direction. Captains and senior leadership can also play a vital role by constantly taking the pulse of the team and each individual player. I often meet with the seniors to work through the best ways to monitor team dynamics and the individual care of players. We divide up the underclassman team members among the seniors. Each senior is responsible for staying in close dialogue with his group of players, encouraging, challenging, motivating, and helping them to process disagreements or concerns they might have.

I have invested time into training seniors to be this type of leader because I am extending a great deal of responsibility to them. This is a win-win situation. The seniors are deeply invested in the team as they recognize how important it is for them to model good leadership. They also have a clear vision of their role to help to shape, guide, and lead the team. Underclassmen feel valued and supported by the seniors. The team dynamics are strong as the players work together. If an assistant coach or I need to be brought into an issue, a senior quickly alerts us. This process produces a culture of incredible self-regulation and accountability.

In the end, clarity on the rules of engagement become a source of great freedom and support. Much of this has to do with the ownership of leadership and the relational emphasis between players and between coach and players.

One of my favorite sayings is "Rules without relationships breed rebellion." Coach Boone recognizes this in *Remember the Titans*. Before they leave camp, he tells his players, "This is no democracy. It is a dictatorship. I am the law."[11] However, he discovers that this military style of leadership cannot compel the guys to like each other. Until they at least respect each other, little can be accomplished. This is why he has players get together, one on one, to tell each other their names and talk about their families. He makes it personal.

When players understand that the rules of engagement have a powerful positive influence on their relationships with each other, with their coaches, and with the work or training they do in their sport, they are well on their way to seeing visions of team success become a reality.

TROPHY PRESENTATION

Before the NBA playoffs began in 2012, Coach Erik Spoelstra presented the Miami Heat with a replica of the Larry O'Brien Championship Trophy. It was made of black ceramic, and everyone on the roster signed it with a gold marker. "It was a commitment we made to each other to do everything it took," LeBron James said.[12] Their ownership of team goals and their commitment to each other paid off. They were able to raise the real Larry O'Brien Trophy after securing the NBA Championship at the end of that season.

PERSONAL EVALUATION/DISCUSSION QUESTIONS

1. Where is your heart with regard to the team's rules of engagement? Are there unresolved issues in your own heart (with coaches or players) that need to be reconciled? What first steps do you need to take to make things right with either a coach or another player?

2. What is your view of your team's "rules of engagement"? Do you view them as restrictive, as intrusions to your life, or as boundaries meant to provide safety and healthy guidance? How is your response to this question pivotal to how you engage with your team?

3. What steps might you take to support and even advance the team's rules of engagement?

4. Where, outside athletics, are you struggling with the rules of engagement? Ask yourself why this is an issue. Examine your heart first, not last. Is there a shift that is needed in your attitude, outlook, or perspective?

How good and pleasant it is
when brothers live together in unity! (Psalm 133:1)

—*Sasha Peters, #1, left midfielder*

CHAPTER FIVE

SO THESE ARE MY TEAMMATES?

"All the believers were one in heart and mind.
No one claimed that any of his possessions was
his own, but they shared everything they had."
—Acts 4:32

HEADLINES

- Team chemistry takes time. Pursue it patiently but relentlessly.
- Successful progression through the stages of team development will advance team chemistry.
- A true team resembles a family.

DON'T FORCE IT

From high school to the professional ranks, no matter the sport or the level of competition, everyone wants to be noticed, recognized, and commended for his or her contributions. Without fail, rookies try to assert themselves to prove that they belong to the new program. They often send a false message that is difficult to pull back once it is out there. There is a fine line to walk between confidence and arrogance, and first impressions are hard to undo. Choose your actions carefully and your words deliberately.

Players respect what you do over what you say you did. Let your play do the talking for you. If you're talented, you won't need to say anything and if you do say something, your words will diminish what you just did. If you are not so talented but are trying to make yourself look better than you are, you will make yourself look worse, losing any respect and credibility among the rest of the players. So if you are talented, speak little. If not so talented, speak less. This is a biblical concept. Proverbs says, "Let another praise you, and not your own mouth; someone else, and not your own lips" (27:2). Growing up I heard a saying that I committed to memory: "It is better to be thought a fool than to open your mouth and remove all doubt." That saying has served me well at times. You too might find it useful in various circumstances.

This principle is not specific to high school athletics. Even in the professional ranks, antics that emphasize the individual get old, and team owners, coaches, and teammates get tired of dealing with players who cause trouble. Think of former NBA power forward, Dennis Rodman, known for his defense and rebounding, NFL wide receiver Terrell Owens, and wide receiver Randy Moss. Each of these three athletes was prolific in his sport. In fact, they were some of the absolute best for their position. However, they were journeymen. They have each played on three or more teams because over time they wear out their welcome. They would have done well to have heeded the words of football coach Lou Holtz: "The freedom to do your own thing ends when you have obligations and responsibilities. If you want to fail yourself—you can—but you cannot do your own thing if you have responsibilities to the team members."[1]

The dynamics of teams are always interesting to observe and assess. Success will hinge a great deal on the effectiveness of a group of talented individuals coming together to strive toward a common goal and to achieve exceptional results. Phil Jackson, coach to the Chicago Bulls, said they won championships because they were "plugged in to the power of oneness instead of the power of one man," referring to the incomparable Michael Jordan.[2] When Jackson took over as head coach in 1989, Jordan had been in the NBA for five years but had not yet won an NBA championship. Jackson stressed to Jordan the importance of making his teammates better around him. He told him, "You've got to share the spotlight with your teammates, because if you don't they won't grow."[3]

Jackson understood what it took for his team to grow, and he pulled Jordan into this discussion to make sure he bought into the team philosophy. Once Jordan did, he led the charge. While coaches are typically interested in this, I have found it helpful to have players understand, identify, and address the stage that our team is in so we can either work to change or to continue in the progress we are making.

When it comes to team development, almost every successful team must press through four specific stages developed by psychologist Bruce Tuckman. I would challenge you to read through these stages in light of Philippians 2:1–4, in which Paul talks about how being united in Christ transforms our way of being with others. Paul challenges us when he says to be

> like-minded, having the same love, being one in spirit and purpose. Do nothing out of selfish ambition or vain conceit, but in humility consider others better than yourselves. Each of you should look not only to your own interests, but also to the interests of others. (Phil. 2:2–4)

STAGES OF TEAM DEVELOPMENT

Stage 1: Forming

At the start of every season, team members are eager to begin. In many ways, they are just getting to know each other. Spirits are high, the work rate is strong, and players are excited to have made the team. However, no games have been played, no major conflict has been encountered, and the team is still unclear as to individual roles and expectations. These must be put in place so the team reaches its true potential and accomplishes its goals.

Stage 2: Storming

During this stage, roles and responsibilities begin to sort out, games are played, and players are pressed in training. Without fail, interpersonal conflicts arise. If a team is ever to come out of this stage, it is vital that the rules of engagement be reviewed, referred to, and followed by all members involved.

It's actually good for a team to find itself in this stage early in the season. Too often conflict is perceived as a bad thing—to the extent that people may avoid dealing with real issues out of fear of conflict. Fear is the greatest obstacle to confrontation. Team members need to coach each other to keep the conflict going until it is resolved. Avoidance can cause team deterioration, leading to a premature ending to the season. Sooner or later, training and games bring out issues that are present just below the surface. Avoidance merely creates an artificial harmony that will prevent the team from functioning well.

When it's properly addressed, conflict is the healthy first step of working together as a team. Dealing with conflict early strengthens the heartbeat of the team. Team members listen to each other, work through their differences, and develop a deeper commitment to the team and to each other.

While we will speak more of communication, there are a couple of important things to keep in mind. If you are in conflict with another, do everything in your power to give them the benefit of the doubt and to think the best of them and their intentions. Also, if you are the one speaking, it is helpful if you have clarity in your own mind as to exactly what your intent is. (Are you trying to be right or be helpful? Are you trying to add to discussion or simply get a point across?)

Stage 3: Norming

In this stage, teams have gone through successful conflict resolution, trust is being built, and team members are beginning to cooperate with each other under the direction and leadership of the coaching staff. As norms for healthy team living are established, a team culture develops and begins to take root. The longer a team successfully operates in such a manner, the greater chance it has of meeting its maximum potential and progressing to the final stage.

There are several important things you can do, as a teammate, to build trust:

1. Be patient. People make mistakes. Don't major in minors. When an environment is safe, mistakes can be great learning tools.
2. Listen more than you talk. Listening builds trust as you show teammates that you value them and what they have to contribute.
3. Do what you say you will do. Broken promises are trust breakers.

Stage 4: Performing

In this stage, the team is highly productive and has learned how to maximize individual and team strengths and to compensate for individual and team weaknesses. While conflict may still arise, the difference in this stage is that the team has previously been successful in addressing matters in a non-superficial way. It is able to recognize conflict and deal with attitudes and motives behind the behavior. Almost without fail, overachieving teams will do more than anyone thought possible because they are able to operate in this stage for a considerable period of time. They are purpose-driven teams that do not allow the minutiae of the day to bog them down or hinder them from achieving their goals.

Conversely, very talented teams that should be far more successful, and possibly win championships, may never truly get past the storming phase of team development. On the surface, everything appears fine. However, the attitudes, intentions, and motives that run counter to the team's focus and perspective cut the team to its knees and cause it to fall far short of what it could be. The end result leaves an incredibly sour taste in everyone's mouth because the whole team knows that what could have been was not, primarily due to the players' inability to press through the interpersonal conflicts that held them captive. Some of my teams have failed to come together, and it is profoundly frustrating and deeply disappointing to squander moments that can never again be recaptured.

WE ARE FAMILY!

It's not uncommon for professional sports figures to summarize the experience they have with each other by saying, "We're family." For some of you, this might not seem so great. After all, families fight, siblings have rivalries, and relatives can struggle to get along well. Growing up with three sisters and having three sons of my own, I know how tough family dynamics can be. However, in my own family's experience, the struggles and tough moments have actually drawn us closer together. The "storming stage" of a family has the potential to divide or solidify family members' commitment to each other. If everyone endures and perseveres, a family can in essence say, "Look at what we've been through. There's nothing we can't press through together now." Instead of pulling apart a family, similar tough situations draw family members together over time. Navigating those good struggles within the safety of the family demonstrates that we can endure the struggles and difficulties that will inevitably come our way.

While all Navy Sea, Air, and Land Teams (SEALs) are trained to operate in any environment, SEAL Team Six (ST6) is the elite of the elite. Of all the Navy SEALs that attempt to become a member of ST6, 75 percent will not even be able to complete the rigorous training.

This team is like none other. The sacrifice is great. SEALs are gone from home at least 200 days of the year. They are trained for any weather, able to use any weapon or operate any vehicle, and will actually endure torture as part of their training to prepare for worst-case scenarios. In the selection process for ST6, trainers do not look for individuals who emerge as leaders; instead they look for those who are the best teammates. One member summed up the depth of the relationships developed when he commented that these men are ready to die for the men next to them.[4]

As a new season begins, do your best to use the talents and abilities that God has entrusted to you. At some point, there will be conflict. When there is, acknowledge that you are in the "storming stage." This stage is not one to run from but one to embrace. Stay in it and be engaged. Look to be part of the solution and not the problem.

This is not an easy task. It may require great humility from you, or it might require you to be the teammate that will hold another teammate accountable for his or her attitude or actions. This is what it means to be a good teammate. Either way, you must move forward even though it feels uncomfortable and awkward in the moment. Passivity and inactivity cannot be options. To take such an approach is to deliberately take a step backward. Individuals and the team will suffer as a result. Embrace those difficult moments, for the reward can be great! James challenges us to view trials with joy.

Consider it pure joy, my brothers, whenever you face trials of many kinds, because you know that the testing of your faith develops perseverance. Perseverance must finish its work so that you may be mature and complete, not lacking anything. (James 1:2–4)

PERSONAL EVALUATION/DISCUSSION QUESTIONS

1. Assess what stage your team is currently in. Is your team progressing forward or is it stuck in a particular stage? Why? (It is important to identify what is going well and what is not to determine what to continue and what to move away from.)

2. How would you characterize the relationships on your team? What about your relationships? Ask others to comment on how they perceive you as a teammate. Find someone who will give you an honest answer and not just a feel-good response.

3. Is there trust among players, and between players and coaches? Discuss your answer. If you conclude that there is trust, what are you basing this on? If you conclude that there is not, why do you arrive at that conclusion and what can be done?

4. What things might prevent your team from moving to the performing stage? What might your role be in helping to bring about a good resolution, should it be necessary?

5. What kind of family would you *like* to say your team resembles? Does it? What conversations do you need to have with your teammates and coaches?

STAGE 2

REGULAR SEASON

"We're going to relentlessly chase perfection.
We won't catch it, but if we constantly chase it,
we'll achieve excellence." [1]

—*Vinci Lombardi*

"Create a significance for the group, whether it is
an organization, a team, or a company. . . .
Each member must feel he or she is part of something
important, and not just putting in time." [2]

—*Rick Pitino*

The kingdom of heaven is like treasure hidden in a field, which a man found and covered up. Then in his joy he goes and sells all that he has and buys that field. (Matt. 13:44 ESV)

—*Josh Powell, #10, midfielder*

CHAPTER SIX

THIS *IS* "NEXT YEAR"

"Forget the former things; do not dwell on
the past. See, I am doing a new thing!
Now it springs up; do you not perceive it?"
—Isaiah 43:18–19

HEADLINES

- Lessons from the past will give clarity to the new season.
- Total team investment is required when setting a course for the new season.
- Count the cost. Are you willing to pay the price?
- Hold an "I get to" attitude instead of an "I have to" attitude.
- Determine where you are going and how you will get there as a team.
- Know and embrace your individual role.

LAST SECOND HEROICS

"There is always next year" is a hated phrase no true competitor ever wants to hear. It is often offered as some sort of condolence, typically after a season-ending loss in a game you should have won. Instead of healing the pain of defeat, being reminded that you have played the final game of the season is like having salt poured into a fresh wound.

In the 2011 Women's World Cup when the United States defeated Brazil, the look on the faces of the Brazilian players said it all. In that match, the U.S. team had to play down a player for the last fifty-five minutes after one of their defenders was given a red card and removed from the match. As the game went into overtime, Brazil scored and seemed to be heading to the championship match. However, the U.S. team refused to quit before the last whistle. During the final minute of stoppage time due to injuries, Abby Wambach drove a header over the outstretched hand of the goalkeeper. Seconds later the game went to a penalty kick shootout. All five of the U.S. players made their penalty kicks, and goalkeeper Hope Solo provided one stop—all the United States needed to secure this improbable, come-from-behind victory! While the U.S. players celebrated with U.S. flags draped about their shoulders, TV cameras caught shots of the Brazilian players staring off into the distance as if in shock and complete unbelief of what had just happened. For them, the phrase "there is always next year" would certainly sound sickening. They had lost a game they should have won, on the grandest stage of women's soccer.

Having lost two soccer state championships on penalty kicks, I personally know that the bitter taste and the sting of defeat can linger for some time. Yet time, coupled with a new season, also provides healing. With this new opportunity comes the excitement of what can be.

A new season is never completely new, however. While new players are always added to the team, typically a core group returns the next year. It's important for these players to spend time reflecting on, assessing, and evaluating the past year in light of the new season. They should begin by asking questions of themselves as individuals. Then team members should have a large-group discussion in which all are willing to ask difficult questions and even more willing to dig for answers and solutions. Let me warn you: this will not be easy, but it will be good!

ASK THE RIGHT QUESTIONS

I suggest that you begin by asking questions that will cause you to focus on many of the positive aspects of the past year. Take out a piece of paper and write out your answers. Get your thoughts in front of you.

To stimulate your thinking, here are some good questions for reflection:

- What was our best game last year? Why was it our best game? What did I/we do well in that game?
- Why did I/we have the success I/we experienced this past year? (Focus on the positive aspects first.) What were the contributing factors for that success?
- Evaluate personal attitude, effort, motives, preparation from preseason, and training sessions all the way through to the end of the year. It will take some deliberate effort on your part to truly reflect on these critical areas. Ask yourself where you did well in these areas.
- What kind of teammate was I? How did I bring out the best in my teammates? Did I view my teammates as competitors who were out to take my playing time? How did I help to develop the players around me?
- Was I a coachable player willing to do what my coach asked of me?
- What was the best thing I offered to my teammates this past season?
- What is my best memory from this past season? Why is it the best?

As you reflect on many of the good things from last season, it's important for you to write them down and keep them in front of you. It might provide you with a different perspective from the one you had during the previous season. Too often we only focus on the outcome, especially when the last game we played didn't have the desired result. However, in many ways we may have had a sweet season.

Now reflect back on the season and ask the more difficult questions. While this may be less enjoyable, it is an equally important exercise that may shape or change the direction that your team must take. Below are some questions for reflection. Be sure to record your responses.

- Once again evaluate personal attitude, effort, motives, preparation from preseason, training sessions, and so on, all the way through to the end of the year. It will take some deliberate effort on your part to truly reflect on these critical areas. Ask yourself where you could have done better in these areas. Be specific and honest with yourself.
- How could I have been a better teammate? What did I have to offer that I withheld?
- How did I respond to setbacks during this past season?
- Where did I hold back or refuse to risk my best (training, being coachable, developing relationships with teammates and coaches, admitting mistakes, being honest with myself)?
- Where could I have helped to make our team or "family" function better?

While there may be many more important questions to consider, hopefully these few will get you openly and honestly reflecting on last season. Notice that I asked very little about outcomes. Instead, almost every question was about process. Only focusing on results will benefit you little. You and your team may have played a brilliant last match that just didn't go your way. This is the beauty and the heartbreak of athletics. Mike Krzyzewski, coach for the Duke University men's basketball team, once said, "Our goal is not to win. It's to play together and to play hard. Then, winning takes care of itself."[1] If you have ever watched the Blue Devils play, you know that they play great team basketball, play extremely hard, and as a result win a great number of games.

If you and your teammates are able to spend serious time reflecting on the past season, I firmly believe you will learn much from this exercise that will dramatically propel you and your team forward. It will keep you from making the same mistakes, will identify areas in your life that need to be addressed, and will allow you to ask yourself questions like the ones listed below:

- Where do we want to go?
- Why do we want to go there?
- How will we get there?
- Does everyone want to go there?
- Do we even have what it takes to get there?
- Are we willing to offer up what it takes to get there?
- What are the first steps we need to take to get there?
- How do we make sure we don't fall into the same mistakes we made during the past season?
- How will we deal with setbacks this season since they are bound to happen?
- What must I surrender for the team to reach its desired destination? Everyone will pay a price. There will be a cost. What am I willing to invest?

Once you and each team member have personally wrestled with these tough questions, you'll be ready to make the road map for your journey. Know that this can be a time-consuming and tedious task. However, not only is it extremely rewarding, it is an absolute must! John Wooden said, "You must never stand still. You're either moving upward a little bit or you're going the other way. You can't expect to go upward too quickly, but you can be sure to go down quickly. The slide down happens in a hurry. Progress comes slowly but steadily if you are patient and prepare diligently."[2]

As you think of your team and what goals it should set for the season, there are a couple of very important things to keep in mind.

Your Input Is Required—Invest!

Too often a small group of individuals establish goals or the direction for the team. This can be helpful, but their vision must extend to the rest of the team. Please do not get me wrong. I firmly believe in leadership and am convinced that a team *without* a visionary coach and strong leadership from within will struggle to reach its full potential. It's very useful for some people to cast a big vision of what the team can do while also understanding the steps all members must take.

Before setting goals, however, every team member must know that his or her voice is not only important but also absolutely needed. Everyone must engage in the process. There can be no fence-sitters or players who refuse to engage in the process. Whether in a high school or college team, all players, freshmen to seniors, must participate. The discipline and commitment required to accomplish team goals requires complete buy-in from every member associated with the team! Passivity in the goal-setting session leads to a lackluster approach to the hard work that will be required.

During our 2011 soccer state championship season, I had a saying for how we would approach training: "Every player, every position, every play, every time." Every player learned what was required from every position, learned what plays needed to be run from those positions, and learned how to execute them every time he was asked. This was an extremely high standard. Without a doubt it pressed many players' commitment levels. However, everyone bought into this approach, and it absolutely paid off.

During that season, we had more injuries than I've ever had on any of my teams in eighteen years of coaching. I had forwards playing on the back line, pulled a midfielder to train him as a goalkeeper, and played with almost every other odd combination you could think of. However, the players' commitment to this approach and to learning the system for every position allowed us to make changes almost seamlessly. All the players knew and bought into this standard. When I was talking to the defenders, my players knew I was talking to everyone because anyone might end up playing that position.

If you are on a team, you cannot afford not to listen and learn everything possible about your entire team's goals and objectives. If you only focus on the position you might be playing, you will be grossly shortsighted. At some point that attitude will greatly hurt the team's opportunity for success.

Count the Cost

In order to become his follower, Jesus said in the Scriptures that you must first "count the cost." He gives two examples to illustrate his point (Luke 14:28–33). The first is of a builder. Before he even lays the foundation, a builder considers whether he has enough money and materials to finish the project. The second illustration is of a king who is ready to go to war against a king with twice as many soldiers. In the same way, Jesus says that to be his disciple and follow after him, a person must be willing to forsake everything he or she has, including the security and familiarity of home and family.

In Matthew 16:25–26, Jesus says,

> For whoever wants to save his life will lose it, but whoever loses his life for me will find it. What good will it be for a man if he gains the whole world, yet forfeits his soul? Or what can a man give in exchange for his soul?

The apostle Paul understood the cost of discipleship and following Jesus. He enjoyed great prominence among the Jewish elite but walked away from it all for the love of Jesus! Paul declared,

> Whatever was to my profit I now consider loss for the sake of Christ. What is more, I consider everything a loss compared to the surpassing greatness of knowing Christ Jesus my Lord, for whose sake I have lost all things. I consider them rubbish, that I may gain Christ and be found in him, not having a righteousness of my own that comes from the law, but that which is through faith in Christ—the righteousness that comes from God and is by faith. (Phil. 3:7–9)

In 1 Corinthians 6:20, Paul reminds us that we were "bought at a price" (the blood of Christ) and tells you to "honor God with your body." This perspective puts the emphasis of counting the cost in an entirely different light. When I consider the sacrifice Christ made on our behalf, I am compelled to believe that if we are going to pursue any good endeavor as Christians, we ought not to give a halfhearted effort.

The apostle Paul was beaten, stoned, shipwrecked, and more. Yet he declared that this suffering was all worth it for the opportunity to know Christ and him crucified. Paul counted the cost by investing his very life, even to his death!

You may be thinking that I'm going overboard when I start talking about life and death issues. Remember our focus. I'm not talking about winning a game but something much bigger than that. I am talking about how to pursue life. If you are going to be involved in sports, then go for it. Don't give a halfway effort. *Middle ground, halfway, partially involved,* or *somewhat committed* are words and phrases that just don't work . . . anywhere in life. On the front end of your season, as you set goals, jump in with both feet.

I would compare it to bidding for something on eBay. Before you begin the bidding, you need to decide in your mind how much you are actually willing to invest, and in order to get your desired result, you will spend to your maximum limit to secure the item you are bidding on. In the same way, ask yourself what you are willing to offer to your sport. I've had players come to me before the season, which is the time to do it, and tell me that they are not committed enough to try out for the team that year. I always hear this with mixed emotion. I hate to hear this because it means we won't be spending quality time together as player and coach in the way we did the year before. At the same time, I absolutely respect and appreciate this personal assessment of where they are, particularly at that point in the season.

Every player must count the cost and determine if he or she is willing to pay the price. Few players see the struggle as giving value to the prize. This is where a shift in mind-set must occur, for the struggle is a beautiful thing. While rarely enjoyable, it must always be embraced! It's easy to look at hard work from a "get by" perspective. Many will do only the minimum required of them. Unfortunately, this is human nature.

This practical example may help to give you a quick self-analysis of where you are. If your coach asks you to do a repetition of a particular skill, what do you do if you finish before the others? It's not uncommon for me to hear this: "Coach, I've finished the ten reps you asked me to do—now what?" When you say this, you imply that you have mastered that skill set. If your coach has not moved you to the next skill set, keep doing it. Try to perfect the skill he or she is trying to teach you.

Some players see hard work as a means to accomplish their goal. The great players see this and more. They see the work as something to revel in! Roy Anderson, a center back from my 2011 state championship team, saw hard work as something he got to do, not something he had to do. This specific mind-set can and must be trained, as we'll see in chapter nine. Roy considered work a privilege or opportunity. It didn't matter what I planned for training each day. For him it was never enough. He always wanted more, always ran to a challenge, and always loved every minute of it. He got it!

This attitude affected every area of Roy's life. During the winter of 2010, bad weather closed our school during the winter finals weeks. As a result, the students had opportunities to opt out of exams. If they wanted to take their exams, their grade would count toward their semester average. Otherwise, the semester grade would be final without their final exam grade. A large majority chose to opt out. However, I will always remember watching Roy walk in the front doors of school with only a handful of other students, sporting a huge grin on his face and exclaiming how excited he was that he had the *opportunity* to take his English exam that day. For him, this was simply a way of life.

Roy's attitude was contagious to those around him. In fact, I could tell who the true competitors were by how they responded to him. True competitors were willing to count the cost and do what was necessary to improve themselves.

Not only that, but they found Roy's enthusiasm motivating and desired to be around him. Others found his enthusiasm to life in general to be over the top because it represented too much work. Such an approach to life is either attractive or repelling. You will run to it or away from it. But beware! What you choose to do has ramifications for the patterns you are establishing for life. Run toward character building and shaping opportunities, not away from them.

John Wooden understood what it meant to be a true competitor. He once said, "The hard struggle is to be welcomed, never feared. In fact, when you define success that way, the only thing to fear is your unwillingness to make the full, 100 percent effort to prepare and perform at the highest level of your ability."[3] When it came to the competition, Wooden said,

> True competitors derive their greatest pleasure out of playing against the very best opponents, even though they may be outscored. The difficult challenge provides rare opportunities to be their best. Often great competitors don't quite have the physical skills of more gifted players, but they get more out of what they have at moments of great pleasure. Thus, I base my judgment on not just what they had but how they used it. To what extent did they attempt to bring forth their abilities? To what extent did they accomplish that under maximum pressure?[4]

Michael Jordan was right when he said,

> You can't turn it on and off like a faucet. I couldn't dog it during practice and then, when I needed that extra push late in the game, expect it to be there. But that's how a lot of people approach things. And that's why a lot of people fail. They sound like they're committed to being the best they can be. But when it comes right down to it, they're looking for reasons instead of answers.[5]

The great Boston Celtic center Bill Russell also understood true discipline. He was such a perfectionist that he would keep his own scorecard for each game. His standard was ridiculously high: twenty-five rebounds, eight assists, eight blocks, and 60 percent field-goal percentage. He graded himself from one to one hundred. In 1,200 games, he never scored higher than a sixty-five.[6]

College basketball coach Bob Knight summed up this idea well when he said, "Self-discipline is doing what has to be done; doing it when it has to be done, doing it the best it can be done, and doing it that way every time you do it."[7]

WHERE ARE WE GOING?

Setting goals comes in two parts. The first has to do with a vision of what you believe you and the team can accomplish. The second part of goal setting has to do with a set of specific, time-sensitive, measurable steps to achieve the dream you set out to pursue.[8]

Every coach handles goal setting differently. As coach, I simply "set the table" for the players. This means I give the players parameters and then have them set their goals as a group. We talk about the past year both in terms of the team's successes and setbacks. I give them my perspective on the team's strengths and weaknesses and the hurdles we must overcome. After this brief overview, I tell the players that I will coach them according to their goals. Then I and the other coaches step out of the room, leaving the captains to lead the meeting.

At this point, all players must be engaged and involved. Total team commitment is vital. I step into the room every now and then to see if they need to run something past me. However, for the majority of the time, this is a players' goal-setting session. After what is typically a two- to three-hour meeting, they call the coaches back into the room, and the captains tell us about their desired outcomes and emphases for the team.

I then play the devil's advocate and press the players to see whether they truly have considered what it will take and if they truly have counted the cost as a team. Sometimes I need to step back out of the room and let the team have a good wrestling match, sometimes almost literally, with each other. Once every player commits to press toward these agreed-on goals with the others, we print out the list, have everyone sign it, and then make a copy for each player to hang in his room at home so it will always be before him.

As a result of this type of goal-setting session, goals are sharpened, vision becomes clearer, and players begin to buy in and become united around and committed to a common cause. However, the job has just begun for coaches and players alike. Up to this point, goals have been set largely based on outcomes. Little will be accomplished if the focus does not turn to daily, minute-by-minute performance.

HOW ARE WE GOING TO GET THERE?

As a player, the challenge is not to get discouraged by slow personal or team progress. Large visions and big goals require patience and deliberate focus, as well as the accomplishment of many smaller goals. While it is important to keep large goals in front of you, you must be able to break down your goals to the point where you are able to give complete focus to the very next step in front of you. A great example comes from the life of Michael Jordan. For nearly eight years, his scoring averages were all near or above thirty-two points per game. However, he didn't think about this number. Instead he focused on earning eight points per quarter. That seemed like a manageable number; after all, it amounted to four field goals in twelve minutes.[9]

In *Success Is Not an Accident*, Newberry says, "Constantly remind yourself that every opportunity or activity is moving you either closer to the accomplishment of your goals or further away. The clock is always ticking. Nothing is neutral, and every single thing you do—or fail to do—counts!"[10] I am the first to admit that no coach is perfect. However, looking back on the coaches I've had over my lifetime, I realize that they had a big-picture perspective that I failed to see when I was in the middle of training or even a match. I was too focused on myself and what was in it for me. This is not uncommon for an athlete, but this narrow perspective will prevent individuals and teams from reaching their goals. Give your coach the benefit of the doubt, as he or she probably has a good reason for asking you to fill the role he or she is asking you to fill.

GOAL ACHIEVING: SO WHAT IS MY ROLE?

While the coach has a great deal of influence in this process, it is important for you to know and be able to articulate exactly what your role is and how you can contribute to the greater good or goal(s) of the team. If you are not able to clearly articulate what your role is, something absolutely must change. If no change occurs, you very likely will lose interest, your commitment will drop off, and ultimately team chemistry will suffer . . . possibly to the point where the team drops back into the storming phase of team development. I have experienced this firsthand when I was not as clear as I should have been with certain players. It leads to mutual frustration. The players are frustrated because they don't know their place on the team even though they desperately want to be part of the team and its success. I am frustrated because they are not "coming through" as I wish they would. While this is primarily a coach's responsibility, I again stress the importance of asking your coach for role clarification. This is an absolute must! Once your coach has clarified your role, it is important to embrace it. Ownership of your role is key to both individual and team success.

In 1 Corinthians 12:12–31, Paul talks about the members of the body and how each member is absolutely vital in order for the body to properly function. This passage refers specifically to the body of Christ, the church, and how we as Christians must not elevate or debase ourselves based on our role. Every role is important, and the body cannot survive without the service of any particular member. I love how this passage addresses the seemingly weaker or less talented members of the body. Paul says, "The parts [of the body] that we think are less honorable we treat with special honor" (v. 23). The point is clear here. For the team to press toward its goals, its members must be focused on the daily performance required of them as individual players. If you are a team leader who gets a great deal of recognition, it is your job to do your part with humility. Remember that Christ said, "From everyone who has been given much, much will be demanded" (Luke 12:48). Use your talents well. If you get little credit, accolades, applause, or the approval of others, don't lose heart. You role is more important than you suspect. Don't look around and be jealous of what others have. Do your best with the talent you have been given and be ready to be called up at any moment.

In the movie *Rudy*, a young man desperately wants to play for the Notre Dame football team. Despite being too small to suit up, he has the heart of a lion and refuses to quit. At one point in the movie, one of the linemen walks up to Rudy in the parking lot after practice and says, "If you don't cool it out there, you'll get yourself killed." Rudy replies, "If I cool it, I won't be helping you get ready for the games."[11] Rudy understands that he has a vital job to do. He won't make the front page of the sports section, he won't be drafted into the NFL, he won't make the box score, and he won't even dress out (except for one game). However, he trains as if his life depends on it and brings out the best in the starters. This is invaluable for the team. Knowing his role is important, Rudy feels valued and part of the success of Notre Dame football. John Wooden refers to his vital role as the "stone that sharpened the sword . . . the starting lineup."[12]

Yet there is a point in the movie where Rudy begins to listen to the lies that his role is not important, that he is not valued, and that he ought to quit. As he is walking out, his friend catches him and speaks direct and necessary words to Rudy. "You're five foot nothin', hundred and nothin', and you have nearly a speck of athletic ability. And you hung in there with the best college football team in the land for two years. And you're gonna walk outta here with a degree from the University of Notre Dame. In this life, you don't have to prove nothin' to nobody but yourself."[13]

Don't listen to the naysayers around you or the lies that the Devil might whisper in your ear. Do your job and do it to the best of your ability. Colossians 3:23 will help you to keep on center with your role and your perspective: "Whatever you do, work at it with all your heart, as working for the Lord, not for men." On every championship team that I have coached, I can quickly think of players who were never in the limelight. Yet had we not had them on the team, I believe we would not have been as successful, and we certainly would not have been complete without them in the middle of our huddle . . . After all, they were family!

PERSONAL EVALUATION/DISCUSSION QUESTIONS

1. Reflecting on last year, what is the most important lesson for you and for the team to learn as you prepare for a new season?

2. As you worked through the many questions in this chapter, which questions were the most difficult for you to answer? Why? What are you learning about yourself during personal reflection and evaluation?

3. Describe the personal investment you are willing to make this season. What will it cost? Are you willing to pay the price?

4. As you answer question 3, discuss your motivation for such an investment. Do you find your ultimate motivation to be team centered or self centered?

5. At this point in the season, do you know what your role is on your team? Would you and your coach be in complete agreement about that role? If not, what needs to happen?

6. What have you learned from the Scripture passages regarding your role on the team and being a member of a team (counting the cost—Luke 14:28–33, Matt. 16:25–26, Phil. 3:7–9, Eccl. 9:10; members of the body—1 Cor. 12:12–31, Luke 12:48)? How will this understanding better prepare you as you enter the season?

7. Are there areas in your Christian life where you have been unwilling to invest as a follower of Jesus? If yes, what are those areas? What has held you back? What might be the first step toward "losing your life" for Jesus' sake (Matt. 16:25–26)?

But he said to me, "My grace is sufficient for you, for my power is made perfect in weakness." Therefore I will boast all the more gladly about my weaknesses, so that the power of Christ may rest upon me. For the sake of Christ, then, I am content with weaknesses, insults, hardships, persecutions, and calamities. For when I am weak, then I am strong. (2 Cor. 12:9–10 ESV)

—*Adam Ryan, #13, played everywhere*

CHAPTER SEVEN

PRESSING ON

"But you, take courage! Do not let your hands
be weak, for your work shall be rewarded."
—*2 Chronicles 15:7 (ESV)*

HEADLINES

- Setbacks and difficulties are inevitable for every team.
- Most team tensions result from player/coach relationships, disagreements over playing time, and how the team handles winning and losing.
- Every successful team will collectively press through times of storms.

DEALING WITH SETBACKS

In the 2006 movie *Rocky Balboa*, Rocky's adult son is verbally abused and berated by his boss. Rocky does not interfere, but as he and his son go for a walk, he offers words to refocus him. He reminds his son who he is and encourages him to do a serious assessment of the direction he is going.

I'd hold you up to say to your mother, "This kid's gonna be the best kid in the world. This kid's gonna be somebody better than anybody I ever knew." And you grew up good and wonderful. It was great just watching you. . . . But somewhere along the line, you changed. You stopped being you. You let people stick a finger in your face and tell you you're no good. And when things got hard, you started looking for something to blame. . . . Let me tell you something you already know. The world ain't all sunshine and rainbows. . . . Nobody is gonna hit as hard as life. But it ain't about how hard ya hit. It's about how hard you can get hit and keep moving forward. . . . That's how winning is done! Now if you know what you're worth, then go out and get what you're worth. But ya gotta be willing to take the hits and not point fingers saying you ain't where you wanna be because of him, or her, or anybody! Cowards do that, and that ain't you! You're better than that![1]

It's inevitable that in every season, just as in life, things won't always go as you planned. The challenge, as Rocky put it surprisingly eloquently (for him), is to take the hits and move forward. Difficult times will inevitably come during a season. Don't look for excuses or someone to blame. You are in it now. No turning back!

BEYOND LOVING THE GAME

Often there are no immediate answers. I have come to learn that hindsight really is 20/20—and it may not come into focus for quite some time. In the meantime we can simmer and stew and be mad about a particular situation or setback, or we can press forward knowing that if we are patient, the lesson in this may be revealed to us. Quitting or backing down when you are hardest hit is a sure way to miss out on some of the richest and greatest blessings in your life.

Following our 2011 state championship and during the course of our 2012 preseason, six juniors quit the high school soccer program. Each one who met with me used the standard line: "I just don't love the game anymore." I challenged them to identify and verbalize what that statement actually meant. Did they mean they didn't love the actual game, or did they mean they didn't like the fact that they might be on junior varsity or wouldn't get varsity playing time? (We had a veteran team with twelve seniors out of twenty players.) Did they not like how hard they would have to work to try to make varsity? What was it?

For each of them, my greatest concern was that this statement was a cover for something else. Something could be going on inside that was less about the actual sport and more about a character issue they were running from. In athletics and in life, we inevitably come up against walls, hurdles, or obstacles. To come to a wall and refuse to press through or go over it is to be robbed of knowing yourself more fully and receiving the blessings on the other side. It is through adversity that character is born.

MISSED TRYOUT

Avoiding the difficulties in the journey might provide temporary relief, but it will leave you haunted by unsettling questions about your character and person. The first employer I worked for out of college had been an outstanding basketball player. One day he was talking to me about his former basketball playing days and how he had been extended an invitation to a tryout with the NBA Chicago Bulls (pre-Michael Jordan). He pulled out a letter from the Chicago Bulls organization and said, "I never went to that tryout, but I have always wondered what would have happened had I actually gone and given it my best shot." He will never know the answer to that question.

HURDLES THAT MUST BE OVERCOME

Over the years I've seen three major stumbling blocks prevent players from pressing forward to maximize their potential and pour it into the team. Players and teams that are unable to work through these issues will never reach the performing stage of team development. Your perspective on your coach, playing time, and game outcomes are great tests of your character and either cause you to remain in the storming stage or to advance into the norming stage of good team development.

Coach

In my first year as the varsity head coach at Chattanooga Christian School, I was put on the spot by a mother at the parent meeting at the beginning of the year. In front of all the other parents, she asked, "How will you be better than the last coach we had?"

I quickly realized that this was a loaded statement. Any comparison I offered would be used against me as evidence that I was running down the former coach. I refused to be suckered into such a trap. Instead I told her that there are many ways to play soccer as well as many ways to coach soccer. Each coach uses the tactics he or she deems best while maximizing the ability of the players. This doesn't mean that one coach is right and another is wrong. Rather, it comes down to two things. First, each person has his or her own preference and opinion of how the game should be played. Second, the head coach will ultimately be responsible for team decisions. I appealed to this woman and to the other parents to support the coaching staff and me as we sought to do what was in the best interest of the players and the team as a whole.

Coaches desire to bring out the best in players because they desire to see the team succeed. If players are successful, they help the team to succeed. If players find themselves at odds with the coach, they must search their own hearts to see if there are areas where they are holding back, refusing to trust, or refusing to fully surrender and sell out for the team. As long as they do not understand or do not buy into the direction of the team and their individual roles on that team, they will be roadblocks to the team's success.

Most people find it natural to imagine a person leading those under him or her (leading down) and maybe leading peers (leading laterally). That is what a captain does. However, few consider the possibility of *leading up*. This method of leadership is vital to the success of your team.

In order to lead up, you must first do your job and do it well. When a coach sees a player working his or her hardest, doing what is asked, and being respectful, the coach will respect and appreciate it. When the player's name comes to the coach's mind, the coach will have positive thoughts about the player. This is to the player's benefit. You must not be impatient. In time, you will be noticed.

Recognize that *leading up* is different from *sucking up*. Sucking up is ultimately about self and how you can get noticed or receive personal gain. Leading up benefits your coach, your teammates, and yes, it benefits you as an individual player. However, personal benefits should be a by-product of serving others instead of the primary motivation for your actions. This is an attitude and a matter of the heart.

The second step is to be humble. Few coaches find arrogance attractive. Arrogance shows that you think there is nothing to learn and that you are unwilling to be led.

Third, establish a good working relationship with the coach. To influence a coach, you must pursue a good player-coach relationship. Influence and relationship are inseparable.

Finally, you need to discover your coach's preferred style of leadership. If certain things seem very important to your coach, then they should be important to you and the other players as well. For example, if being on time and wearing specific practice gear is important to the coach, consider it important. You will be shocked by the results.

When you do your job well, exceed expectations, act humble, pursue a strong and healthy player-coach relationship with your coach, and study his or her preferred style of coaching and leadership, you will be amazed not only by how you feel toward the coach but also by how positive you will be about your role as a team member.

I'm not guaranteeing that your playing time will increase. In fact, if you do this with playing time as your chief goal, your coach will probably see through to your ulterior motive. Players should be genuine and sincere in attitude and effort. Your coach is not your enemy but rather a great ally and supporter!

Playing Time

If there is one issue that can divide a team in a moment, it is the issue of playing time. Players join a sport to play in games, parents support their athletes and pay both monetarily and with time, and coaches desire to put forward the best team to attain the victory. Tensions and strain mix in with this. Most parents believe that their athlete should play more than he or she does. When asked, most players would say they should get more playing time. Yet, when pressed, players usually know where they stand on the team because practice sessions serve as a daily reminder and measure of exactly where they are.

Let me offer a coach's perspective. This may give you one way to view the issue of playing time and the challenge each coach has. Let's examine a high school varsity basketball team. The game is a total of thirty-two minutes long. Let's say there are twelve players on the team, yet only five can play at a time. If we take the thirty-two minutes and multiply it by five, the total number of minutes that the basketball coach has to work with is 160 minutes. If he or she divided that time evenly among all twelve players, each would receive thirteen minutes and thirteen seconds.

If the coach evenly distributed playing time in this way, just as many would be upset. This strategy would slight the giftedness of image bearers of God. In 1 Corinthians 12, Paul talks about how each person receives different spiritual gifts for different roles and functions. These gifts are to be used for the glory of God and for the benefit and the building up of others. In light of this perspective, consider your own sport and roster size, run the numbers, and ask yourself this question "How much playing time do I realistically believe I should be getting?" Seriously—wrestle with the answer to this question. If a score is being kept on a scoreboard, then winning is a factor. To that end, those most suited for the imposed demands of the game will receive more playing time than others.

I would encourage you to recall the discussions in chapter three regarding your specific role and purpose on a team as defined by the conversations you have had with your coach. If your purpose and role is clear, your earned playing time will make more sense and how you perform during that time will also be more deliberate and focused. If you feel you are getting fewer minutes than you deserve, then your propensity can be to "over-perform" and to act more as an individual and less as a team player in an attempt to impress the coach and prove that you deserve more playing time. Conversely, if your purpose and role are clear, you will perform more freely and will find greater joy. Suddenly mistakes don't become "the end of the world," and accomplishments are a reason for greater celebration when they are for God's glory and for others!

If you are a "star" on the team, I should note that while you have an important role, it is no more important than the role of the player next to you, the coach, or the guy who is regularly on the bench. Wooden used to tell his players, "Everyone has to fill their role for this team to reach its full potential . . . everyone on this team is equally important to the team. Nobody is bigger than the team. Nobody! Remember that."[2]

Winning and Losing

While two upcoming chapters deal specifically with winning and losing athletic contests, there is plenty to be said in this specific context. I have played alongside players who are stone-faced, appearing as emotionless as if they had ice running through their veins. I myself tend to be more . . . let's just say *enthusiastic* when it comes to athletics. While I'm still not great at it, I know I should never get too high or too low. Outcomes don't define you as a person or as a team, contrary to popular belief. Stay focused on the process. As I have mentioned, don't listen to too much praise or too much criticism. Too much criticism is heavy to bear, and great discouragement sets in before long. Too much praise messes not only with your ego but with your work rate. You will begin to think that you do not need to work very hard. Either one messes with your head and your season.

Over the years I have found excessive praise and criticism to be equally damaging. For example, a few years ago, I had three sophomore players that made "best of preps" in Chattanooga. It is rare for people to make this roster at such a young age, meaning these players had established themselves as three of the top soccer players in the greater Chattanooga area. Unfortunately, this was announced at the end of regular season, just before post-season began. I soon saw that the level of praise they were receiving was a bit much for them to handle. Their effort dropped in practice, and they had an air about them that showed they thought they were better than others and didn't need to work as hard. Thankfully, they recognized it and came to me before I went to them. They confessed their lack of effort and poor attitudes and vowed to be better next training session . . . which they were!

When it comes to games, keep things in perspective. Victory belongs to the Lord, and the credit is due to him. So when you receive praise for a job well done, practice offering it back—but now outward and upward to the One who allowed you to be successful in the first place. In chapter thirteen, we will go into much greater detail, but in summary, losing a game can teach incredible lessons. Don't miss the opportunity to learn. A loss that is not followed by evaluation and personal assessment is a far greater loss than the score that appears on some board or in a newspaper.

The following lines come from the poem "Don't Quit":

Often the goal is nearer than
It seems to a faint and faltering man.
Often the struggler has given up,
When he might have captured the victor's cup.
And he learned too late when the night came down,
How close he was to the golden crown . . .

So stick to the fight when you're hardest hit,
It's when things seem worst that you mustn't quit.[3]

PERSONAL EVALUATION/DISCUSSION QUESTIONS

1. What is the one thing (or maybe two things) that you have trouble pressing through in athletics? The obstacle is different for everyone, but it is important to name it in order to address it. Why is this area difficult for you?

2. More than anything else, what causes you to want to quit and throw in the towel? Why? What is behind this conclusion?

3. This chapter marks the middle of the book and well may come at the middle of your season. It is a good time to take inventory and evaluate where you stand with your coach, playing time, and winning and losing. Be honest with yourself! If there is unrest and a disquiet spirit about you, pray about the matter and then speak to your coach. Unresolved, the matter may well get worse! So where are you with these three areas?

Rejoice in the Lord always. I will say it again: Rejoice! Let your gentleness be evident to all. The Lord is near. Do not be anxious about anything, but in everything, by prayer and petition, with thanksgiving, present your requests to God. And the peace of God, which transcends all understanding, will guard your hearts and your minds in Christ Jesus. (Phil. 4:4–7)

—*Cameron Anderson, goalie*

CHAPTER EIGHT

SHOOT STRAIGHT WITH ME

"Reckless words pierce like a sword,
but the tongue of the wise brings healing."
—Proverbs 12:18

HEADLINES

- Good team communication is everyone's responsibility.
- Occasional miscommunication should be expected.
- Your personal initiative is part of the solution.

I AM A PROUD MEMBER of the Red Sox Nation. I was a Red Sox fan long before the team won the World Championship in 2004 and 2007. I grew up in New England. I watched the ball go through Bill Buckner's legs, and I watched the Red Sox go into their late season slump with the mighty Yankees roaring by to clinch yet another pennant. I knew that recurring nightmare all too well.

Then something changed. The Red Sox started to win! Not only did they beat the New York Yankees, but they started to win championships. With championships came expectations. With expectations came high standards. Fans wanted their team to win more championships. Whether it was the pressure to win, complacency because of their nine-game lead with only twenty-four games left to play, or the highly criticized fried chicken and beer in the clubhouse during games, the Red Sox ended the summer of 2011 in a heartrending way! In fact, it was statistically the third worst collapse in baseball history. This once-mighty $161 million franchise subsequently fired the dearly beloved manager who had brought the team not one but two World Series championships.

In short order the Red Sox hired the colorful and animated Bobby Valentine. In early April 2012, Bobby Valentine criticized hardworking fan favorite Kevin Youkilis by questioning his commitment level during a public interview. This act was outrageous to the other players and to Youkilis himself. Youkilis immediately went to his new manager and asked what was going on.

There was no shortage of folks analyzing the situation. The managers could have done many things differently. After all, the manager or coach must lead and set the tone. The style of the team's former manager, Terry Francona, had been to give the players a lot of rope. Unfortunately, they had used it to hang themselves. They needed less rope and more structure. Valentine came to the Red Sox already known for his wild antics and random, unexpected comments.

However, I want to focus on of the actions of Kevin Youkilis. When he began to hear stories swirling about his manager running him down, the first thing he did was speak directly with his coach. Obviously it would have been nice if Valentine had come and spoken to him personally and privately. However, Youkilis did what Youkilis needed to do. He could have brooded over it and created a nightmare with the Boston media, but instead he walked into his manager's office and addressed the matter head-on.

EVERYONE'S RESPONSIBILITY

One of the worst things that can happen on an athletic team, or with any group of people pressing toward a common goal, is for there to be an absence of proper communication between the right individuals. You might think it's the coaching staff's responsibility to initiate good communication and eliminate confusion. Yes, good communication must begin from the top. Absolutely! However, many times as a coach I've thought I was explicitly clear in my communication and expectations, only to find out later that players were scratching their heads in confusion. As a player, what is your role in these situations?

Before we get to solutions, it might be helpful to look at ways communication can be botched. Recognizing such blunders might make the remedy more applicable.

Miscommunication Is Inevitable

I wish I could tell you that miscommunication can be avoided altogether. In reality most conflict in the world begins through some level of misunderstanding between two or more people. If you don't believe me, consider the American Civil War back in the 1800s. If we asked someone in the North and someone in the South during that time, or possibly even today, for the reason for the fighting, both sides would likely offer very different answers.

In the sports world, emotions, the game clock, strong personalities, the drive to win, and stiff competition all collide. That's a perfect combination for a pressure-cooker situation where things will be missed, misinterpreted, or lost in translation. How can this be minimized or avoided?

Let's begin by recognizing that there are many different types of communication. These have different effects for different individuals. Since God made each of us unique, we respond in our own unique ways based on what we hear, think, or think we heard and what we believe the presenter of that information actually intended to communicate. In other words, not just communication can be tricky. A layer of varying interpretations increases the difficulty, giving us a breeding ground for miscommunication. As a result, confusion, frustration, and exasperation can quickly rule the day . . . for *everyone* involved!

The longer I coach the more I have to remind myself that it is not what I say but what players hear that is most important! Sometimes I say one thing while my body language communicates something entirely different. According to the Association for Applied Sports Psychology, 70 percent of human communication is nonverbal.[1] In sports like baseball or softball, this percentage might be even higher, since intentional nonverbal signs are created to communicate in a code that the other team cannot decipher. The reality is that our eye contact, facial expressions, posture, gestures, space, and proximity to those with whom we are in conversation are all factors that contribute to our dialogue.

Don't Wait—Initiate!

So what is a player to do? You may think these topics are for coaches to learn and read about, and you are correct. However, if you are going to be part of a team, you will have to be part of the solution during communication breakdowns. If your coach is like me, then it is vital for you to actively take steps to initiate better communication. Here are some things you should know about me that are probably true of your own coach:

I talk a lot. Proverbs 10:19 says, "When words are many, sin is not absent." That is a sobering verse for me. I know I need to choose my words wisely . . . I just wish I did it more often. At times I wish I could take back some of my words! Sometimes, though, I don't realize this and need others to show me where my blinders are preventing me from seeing important truths. Players can be helpful to me in this area.

I am a sinner, and my intentions are not always right. I might believe my intentions are justified in the moment, but I need the Holy Spirit to expose those areas to me. Proverbs 16:2 says, "All a man's ways seem innocent to him, but motives are weighed by the LORD." I hate to say these next words, but they are so true: I will disappoint my players. I don't want to hurt others with my words or actions but the reality is—I do. I do this with my children and my wife and my coworkers. I hope I am doing this less as I grow in my walk with the Lord and better recognize my wrongdoing and the propensity of my heart. As a coach, I desire to be respected but not revered. Only God should be revered. If you think too highly of me, then you will be more disappointed when my sin comes out.

I want to see growth in my players beyond the athletic arena. Paul gives us a picture of what this should look like as he mentors Timothy. In 2 Timothy 1:2–3, he notes, "To Timothy, my dear son. . . . I thank God, whom I serve . . . with a clear conscience, as night and day I constantly remember you in my prayers." (Chapter fifteen specifically focuses on this point.)

So, if we recognize that yes, coaches talk a great deal, and yes, they make mistakes as sinners, *but* a large majority desire to see players grow and develop on and off the field . . . then what you are thinking and feeling as an individual is vitally important to you *and* to them!

I know none of the following will be easy, but it will be good! When conflict, confusion, or lack of clarity exists due to apparent miscommunication, there are several things you can do and should do as a player.

Respectfully ask your coach for a meeting. It is important to give the coach the opportunity to set up a time that works well for him or her. You don't want to surprise your coach or try to fit in a discussion right before practice is about to begin. You want your coach's single-minded focus on you and the situation at hand. Timing is everything. If you feel you are bringing strong emotion into the situation, you may need to wait twenty-four hours before meeting to allow for a "cooling-off period."

Ask for clarification and listen well. Express where you believe conflict or misunderstanding exists. Lead with questions, not assumptions or accusations. This simple yet vital clarifying approach will be better received than if you throw out conclusions that may or may not be right. As your coach speaks, listen to what said he or she is saying before responding too quickly. Proverbs 18:13 says, "He who answers before listening—that is his folly and his shame."

Repeat back to your coach what you heard. Some starting responses might be "So what I am hearing you say is," "It sounds to me like," and "If I understand you correctly." Clarity must be achieved.

Now, I cannot guarantee that you will like what your coach says. In a similar meeting with my college coach, I did not like it when he told me that my perceived ability exceeded my actual ability and then proceeded to show me a videotape that proved his point. However, at the time I needed that direct and honest feedback. Remember, the issue at hand is clear communication—not necessarily hearing what makes us feel good at the moment!

Respectfully say what needs to be said. Don't leave the meeting with matters unresolved. Yes, this will take courage. If done respectfully, both you and your coach will come away from this time together with a greater appreciation of and respect for the other's perspective.

Finally, lead your coach. In chapter seven I spoke about the importance of *leading up.* In this case, help your coach to coach you. As coaches we understand that we don't coach a team, but we coach individuals on a team. It takes time to figure out how to address individual players and their unique God-given personalities.

Let me illustrate. I had a striker who was extremely talented. However, when I would shout across the field to him, he seemed to melt inside. Over time, this became a matter of frustration for both of us. He didn't like for me to shout across the field because he felt like he was being called out. I was becoming more frustrated because I felt I couldn't communicate with him during a match. During one match the tension mounted until I decided I would substitute him out and talk through the matter right in the middle of the game.

"I'm trying to figure out how to communicate with you during the game, and I need your help," I said. "Here are some options as I see them. I can call across the field to you, I can call you over to the sidelines and we can talk, or I can substitute you out, look you in the eye, and calmly tell you what I think you need to hear and then have you go back into the game. Might any of these solutions work well?"

He said, "Actually if you would do the last one, that would be the best option." So that is how I coached him for the rest of his career.

During that moment, I learned a great deal about that player. If he had not opened up and shared what he was really thinking, our frustration over our communication would only have grown. As lines of communication and expectations for ongoing conversations became clear, we were able not only to finish our time together well as player and coach but today enjoy conversations and life beyond athletics.

Might there be circumstances that are preventing this outcome between you and your coach? It can be different. What conversations need to happen? Don't waste time and possibly endure sleepless nights. Have the conversations that need to take place. You, the coach, and the team will be better as a result.

THE REST OF THE STORY

The 2012 baseball season was a disaster for the Boston Red Sox. Shortly after the Kevin Youkilis situation, he was traded. The Red Sox finished in last place in their division and fired their manager Bobby Valentine. Not much went right for the Boston Red Sox. The communication blunders between players and the team manager were numerous. It does not have to be that way with you, your coach, and your team.

IN THE DRIVER'S SEAT

Recently one of my sons started driving, and I found myself in the passenger's seat. As I listened to myself talk to him about the importance of checking his rearview mirror and side mirrors while always looking ahead, I found great parallels to this topic. In communication, if one looks too far ahead and only ahead, they may miss the present conversation and the benefits of glancing back to see the benefits of either past ground gained in conversations or mistakes made that can be corrected. Balance is crucial. Constantly looking back will cause us to lose sight of what lies ahead and subsequently focus on the wrong conversations in the present or get stuck in conversational ruts that should have faded from view "miles" ago. Like a driver of a vehicle and an athlete on an athletic team, a 360-degree view of communication is vital.

PERSONAL EVALUATION/DISCUSSION QUESTIONS

1. Identify areas or possible scenarios of frustration that you have experienced in athletics over the years that are due to communication breakdowns.

2. How have you handled these communication breakdowns in the past?

3. If similar circumstances were to present themselves again, what might you do differently? How might the five-step process of a healthy meeting with your coach change the outcome?

4. Maybe there is a communication problem between you and another player on the team. How might you *lead laterally* and address the issue with that player? How might you help to bring about reconciliation or restoration?

Since we have these promises, [God is our heavenly father, and we are his sons] dear friends, let us purify ourselves from everything that contaminates body and spirit, perfecting holiness out of reverence for God.
(2 Cor. 7:1)

—*Nick Russell, #21, right midfielder*

CHAPTER NINE

WINNING THE HEAD GAME

*"I can do everything through him
who gives me strength."*
—*Philippians 4:13*

*"Therefore, prepare your minds for action; be self-
controlled; set your hope fully on the grace to be
given you when Jesus Christ is revealed."*
—*1 Peter 1:13*

HEADLINES

- Mental or psychological training is as important as physical training.
- Thoughts planted in our minds govern our attitudes and actions.
- We can control our mental training and toughness.
- Deliberate steps can and must be taken to maximize our mental capacity.

MENTAL OVER PHYSICAL

Pick a season, pick a sport, pick a team . . . no matter what you choose, you will find pages and pages of examples in which the mental aspect of the game determines the outcome. Elements of many team sports come down to what seems like nonaction compared to the rest of the sport. In a football game, bodies crash and fly around, but the game can be won or lost in the last second because of a single kick of a ball through two posts—a field goal. In soccer, a team can play to a 0–0 tie after 120 minutes of exhausting effort, and the game can come down to someone kicking a stationary ball twelve yards past a goalkeeper into a goal twenty-four feet wide and eight feet high. In baseball or softball, a team can be tied after nine or more innings, yet a pitcher who loads the bases can lose the game by throwing four balls to the batter. The batter can become a hero without ever swinging the bat, as he or she trots down to first and the person on third walks to home plate for the "walk off" run. A game of basketball can be determined by a free throw, and there is nothing the other team can do to defend the shot. The list goes on and on.

What binds these last-minute victories and defeats together? The closing seconds of the game are the most intense and action filled of the entire contest—even though the necessary action may appear very simple. The greatest action required is invisible to the naked eye, lying deep in the minds and the hearts of the athletes who step into that arena. For them, these may be the most action-packed, heart-pounding, adrenaline-rushing moments of their athletic career. If this were not so, coaches would not call timeouts whenever possible in order to "ice" the opposing player. It's not that a player steps into the spotlight only to suddenly forget what must be done or lose the skills required to do it. No, the question is: can he or she do the job under intense pressure? Will the individual be able to perform when the team, fans, and possibly even the season are riding on that one moment?

FRESHMEN COURAGE

In 2009, our team was in the state tournament. We had played through regulation, overtime, and sudden death but were locked in a 1–1 tie. During the penalty kick (PK) contest, both teams went through their first five PK kickers. This meant each coach had to select one player from each team for PK sudden death. We did this two times—still tied.

By this point, the game had lasted nearly three hours. We had prepared for this moment in practice, but the next guy to take the PK suddenly began to cramp up and didn't feel able to come through. Sensing the mounting tension, my players were not overly excited about stepping into that pressure-cooker situation.

This was not the time to select a player. Whoever kicked the ball had to believe in himself in that moment, otherwise our success was unlikely. "Guys," I said, "I need someone to step up and take this kick . . . and I need someone now."

Silence followed my request. Moments later, a young freshman suddenly said, "I gotcha, coach! I can make this!"

I wish I could tell you that he stepped up and scored the winning goal and that we carried him off the field as a hero. He did step up and strike a great ball. It was going into the upper corner but caught the underside of the crossbar and shot straight down without crossing over the goal line. We ended up losing that match. The young man was devastated, but the entire team sprinted to him and our goalie to assure them that we win and lose as a *team*.

Consider what happened in this young man's head and what action he took as a result. No one present failed to understand the pressure of that kick. It is one thing to be an observer of an intense match but quite another thing to actually be the "man in the arena" doing what no one else wants to do in that moment. Three years after the match, I still have great regard and respect for this young freshman, who, with ice running through his veins and his mind steady, stepped up and said, "I gotcha, coach!" To him I say,

"Well done, Clark! I am proud of you for stepping forward in that moment!"

"PLAYER OF THE WORLD"

Most athletes operate and accomplish far less than their capacity or potential would allow because they are not tapping into a resource that lies deep within them. Athletes spend hours and hours getting physically fit, yet spend almost no time preparing to be mentally fit. Recently *Sports Illustrated* came out with an article on the Barcelona soccer team titled "The World's Team." A great deal of the article focuses on Lionel Messi, currently known as the greatest soccer player. He is the most prolific scorer in Europe and three times has earned the Player of the World award! The interviewer asked Messi's teammates, "What do you see in Messi that impresses you the most?" One responded:

> The hardest thing in soccer is to take on the defender and dribble around him. . . . Well, Messi dribbles around four, five, six, seven and scores. That's practically impossible today. . . . In a combination play you can get there, but he does it by himself and does it in each game. In soccer there are two speeds: physical, the speed of your legs, and mental. . . . He has both. That's why he's the best in the world.[1]

REAP WHAT YOU SOW

The essence of mental toughness can be explained by the simple analogy of a farmer planting his crops and harvesting what he plants. If I plan corn seeds, I won't find watermelon suddenly growing in my field. In the same way, the things I choose to plant in my head will germinate and grow. In the end, I will reap the benefits or consequences of allowing certain thoughts to enter and remain in my head.

Every day certain thoughts pop up. Thoughts enter and exit all day long as though our minds have swinging doors. However, some take residency in our minds. They set up camp, and we allow them to hang around . . . sometimes for a very long time. These thoughts influence our behavior as we live from the inside out. We control which thoughts we allow to linger and remain, and the thoughts we dwell on or even fixate on will govern us.

This means we should be awfully picky about which thoughts we allow to camp in our minds, because they determine our attitudes and actions. It takes deliberate training to focus our minds in such a manner. While the author is unknown, the poem below drives home the crucial importance of how our thoughts dictate our actions.

If you think you are beaten, you are;
If you think you dare not, you don't.
If you'd like to win, but think you can't
It's almost a cinch you won't
If you think you'll lose, you're lost,
For out in the world we find
Success begins with a fellow's will;
It's all in the state of mind.
If you think you're outclassed, you are.
You've got to think high to rise.
You've got to be sure of yourself before
You can ever win a prize.
Life's battles don't always go
To the stronger or faster man;
But sooner or later the man who wins
Is the one who thinks he can.[2]

Your athletic potential, opportunity, and outcomes will be determined in large part by what goes on inside your head. Let me give you an example. It was always thought that no one could break the four-minute mile barrier. Runners had conditioned their minds to believe it could not be done . . . except one man. In 1954 Roger Bannister believed he could break the sub-four-minute mile barrier. He set his mind to it and shocked the world with his success! Suddenly all other top runners had a mind shift. The thought they had dismissed began to camp in their heads—maybe they too could break the four-minute mile mark. Since 1954, thousands have broken the four-minute barrier, and the record has been broken sixteen times. Moroccan runner Hicham El Guerrouj set the current record on July 7, 1999, when he ran a mile in three minutes and forty-three seconds.[3]

WHAT DO YOU SENSE?

In chapter six, we talked about setting both outcome and process goals. Training for mental toughness is no different. You must envision where you want to be and believe you can get there. I used to think this whole visualization and mental focus thing was overrated and that all I needed to do was be a fitness machine. How immature of me. God gave us our bodies, yes, but our minds act as the captain of the ship, setting the course it will take. The more I studied and practiced mental training, the more I saw its great benefits. If you are a glass-half-empty type of person, know this will be very difficult for you—but not impossible. Keep this in mind: the greatest tool available to you is your mind. It is at the core of any good athletic accomplishment.

As a high school men's varsity coach, my career coaching record is 321–61–25. Of all those games, I can think of six that I did not think we would win. We certainly lost more games than those six, but we certainly never won the games I as a coach had written off as a loss. Obviously you can't just "think it" and victory is sure, but if you don't think positively, you are greatly limiting your chances.

Begin with outcome-based mental training through all your senses. When you think of your goals, what do your senses tell you? Where do they take you? For myself, I see the crowds gathering; I see the state championship stadium and the field; I smell the recently cut bermuda grass; I touch the trophy set on a stand where all the teams can see what they are playing for. Then my vision begins to narrow. I see my team walking in two lines onto the field, warming up, then gathering in the huddle, looking into each other's eyes with obvious nerves . . . but then the first whistle blows. All preparation is now in the past. This moment is about defending that turf like our home field, attacking and driving goals into the back of the net. I watch the game end with our team walking across the field arm in arm while the announcer declares us state champs. We hoist the trophy above our heads.

As a player, break this vision down to your sport and your role. What do you see? What do you think, say, and imagine to yourself? If your thoughts, feelings, emotions, and self-talk are all negative, you will struggle to find success or achievement. Losers are negative; winners are positive. Winning is ultimately the result of self-fulfilling prophecy . . . unfortunately, so is losing.

Losing usually comes in the form of being unsuccessful in the little things that ultimately make a big difference. Let me illustrate. Some years ago, I worked with a very talented forward who was erratic in his performance. When he was dispossessed of the ball early in a tough match, he would begin to fold and give up. Noticing this, I knew something other than physical fittness or lack of talent was the issue. As we debriefed and I asked him about his self-talk, he began to tell me not only the negative things he said in his head but those things he would actually tell the defenders around him. He would say, "I'm terrible; I can't ever get by you" and "I suck; I can't play this position." He was right. Once he mentally sabotaged himself, deciding in his mind and verbalizing to the players he was opposing that he was a failure, the internal and subsequent external battle was over. He was the victim of his own wobbly mind.

When I talk about winning and losing, I am not specifically talking about the scoreboard. A winner can lose on the scoreboard, yet view the loss as a learning experience to grow from. That player will, at some point, reap great benefits from such an outlook.

GIGO EFFECT

If you have a vision of what can be, then you can envision the steps of action necessary for accomplishing these goals. Mind training is not a one-time event. You must revisit your vision often since the mind trains and controls the body. If you miss this point, you will always come up short. Coaches throw around sayings such as "get your mind in the game," "mind over body," "mental preparation," or "mental focus" that all come down to this main idea.

You can't just throw on your shoes or cleats minutes before the game and expect results. Think back to Mia Hamm, who told her coach that she wanted to be the best soccer player in the world. Obviously that goal or outcome is not for everyone. Yet even Hamm had to break it down to a process of mental training. I guarantee there were days when she did not want to practice or do the extra work required. However, she had trained her brain to overrule the negative thoughts that popped into her head. She had worked on outcome-and-process mental training so that those overriding thoughts in her head were so cemented that they were nearly unmovable.

Most of us react to each passing thought or whim that pops into our heads. As a result, our discipline, mental focus, and preparation are severely lacking. In his book *Playing Out of Your Mind*, Alan Goldberg refers to this as the "GIGO Effect." GIGO stands for Garbage In, Garbage Out.[4] What you put in your body physically affects your play. Once during an indoor soccer match, one young man told me he had just come from a fair and had eaten cotton candy, ice cream, loads of candy and wasn't feeling good—but wanted to play. Not more than ten minutes into the game, he threw up all over the indoor artificial turf. What a mess!

In the same way, the negative thoughts we put in our minds have the same effect. In short order, we will in essence start "vomiting" out a negative response that will reveal that we have lost the mind game. If we expect to have good results, we must plant good thoughts to germinate and be harvested in our minds. Mental toughness at its best is able to block out anything that is not important. You can be guided in this way, but this matter must be settled by you! Coach yourself well!

STEPS FOR MENTAL TRAINING

Although I could dedicate the rest of this book to this topic, allow me to provide some concise key overarching thoughts about mental preparation and mental toughness training. Don't skip over this section too quickly. Take out a sheet of paper and begin a self-evaluation as you go through each statement. If you are honest with yourself and really wrestle with your answers, this mental exercise will be comparable to playing an athletic contest that leaves you exhausted. However, this training causes your physical training to be more purposeful.

Know where you want to go and don't compromise. Always keep the big picture at the front of your mind. Much has been said of this already. What is your personal "four-minute mile" that you or others have thought could not be accomplished?

Break your big picture vision and goals into manageable steps. As it's been said, "Inch by inch, anything is a cinch; yard by yard, it might be hard." Or, as the cliché goes, "Rome was not built in a day." Make sure your steps are challenging and specific, with measurable goals that are directly tied to your desired outcomes or your big-picture vision. Allow for adjustments as circumstances permit. Put your goals down on a calendar. Look at it daily. For example: *As a basketball player, I will work on my ball-handling skills for twenty minutes, four times a week.*

Document your successes. If you don't focus on your short-term gains, you risk discouragement, forcing your mind to work overtime to stay mentally strong.

Be self-motivated. If you need someone or something to get you "up" for a training session or a game, that ought to tell you about your lack of mental toughness. For example, players who need loud music to get pumped up are essentially saying, "On my own I can't get where I need to go mentally, so I use this extrinsic motivator to ramp me up." What happens when your motivator is not accessible to you one day? Consider spending time in solitude visualizing the game—moment by moment. Try walking through the stages and places of a game and thinking of how you might respond. Review your process goals and how you have trained for specific moments.

Closely monitor your vocabulary. You will have to eliminate words like *can't, won't, impossible, never,* etc. Remember not to limit this to the spoken word, but also guard against the negative thoughts that creep into your head. Don't let them set up residency there!

Surround yourself with positive people. This will be difficult—there are more naysayers in this world who can find every reason to avoid life's slight discomforts. The world is also full of those who love to see successful people fail. Sometimes they present themselves to you as friends and supporters. Jealousy is a horrible thing! You will need encouragers who believe in you and where you hope to go.

Practice taking risks. Those who are willing to fail repeatedly in practice eventually find success in the contest. You have to let go of your mistakes very quickly. During a contest, no one is going to counsel you through your moments of difficulty or disappointment. You can do nothing about the past but learn from it, so move on and learn . . . and do so as quickly as possible.

I regularly tell my players that the most important thing they do with a mistake is the very next thing. Unfortunately for some, the very next thing is to pout, sulk, shake, or hang their heads. Your mental toughness is visible in how you respond directly after a mistake. Players who regularly do the next best thing possible immediately after making a mistake are some of the most mentally tough players.

Think of obstacles as opportunities! For most people, obstacles are game changers. For the opportunist, walls are for hurdling, roadblocks are for going around, and the end of the road is a chance to forge a new path. If someone tells you that you can't do something or that you will never be able to (fill in the blank), how do you respond in such situations? Be careful not to let others take over your mind and course of action.

Do the work! Nothing, I mean nothing, takes the place of what we affectionately refer to on our team as "good hard work." *Persistent, diligent,* and *persevering* must be words you associate with who you are as a person. This idea weds together mental and physical training. The longer games go on, if you are physically fit, you will be able to look your opponent in the eye and go toe to toe knowing you can outlast them. If you are not fit, your body will be screaming so loudly that your mind will relent. If you are pressed hard to succeed in physical training, you will simultaneously grow in mental training.

Believe in yourself! If you don't believe in yourself, who will? If you do believe in yourself, you will take risks and experience success.

Focus on the process. This may be one of the hardest obstacles to overcome. The process is what you have control over. Too often we tie outcomes to ability; you can compete at the top of your game and still be beaten. Conversely, you can win and play poorly. I have seen plenty of both. After competition, focus on what you can do to improve—regardless of the outcome. Mentally weak athletes will not spend much time thinking about this after a win, as their shortsighted focus is on having just achieved the desired outcome.

For example, if you are not getting the playing time you think you deserve . . . then maybe your coach is right and you really don't deserve it. In other words, your focus has to stay steady regardless of the perceived setbacks. Don't shift all your focus to playing time. Focus on improving skills that will get you in the match. Most coaches will have their best players play.

Balance your nerves. In education, we talk about people's "level of concern." For example, if I assigned a two-page paper and told the class it was due in two months, the level of the students' concern would be so low that almost no one would begin the paper. However, if I assigned a ten-page paper and said it was due the next day, the level of concern would be so high that students would be freaking out, throwing fits, and panicking. Most would not even attempt the assignment.

The same is true in athletics. If players approach a game with a ho-hum attitude, their performance likely will be subpar. Often this careless approach emerges when the other team is of a lesser caliber, which is why a lesser, more focused team can defeat a more talented, less focused team. Conversely, if your nerves are so amped up and you are off the charts "jacked up" for a game, you will expend valuable nervous energy before the game even begins.

Each person is different. The best way to know yourself is to journal after games where the opponent was strong and not so strong. Journal after games where you played well and not so well. Start by asking yourself why you played well, why you didn't, and what the contributing factors were. How did you handle pre-game? When did you arrive at the field or court? What did you do before the game began? How did you respond to setbacks during the game?

> "Therefore we do not lose heart. Though outwardly
> we are wasting away, yet inwardly we are being
> renewed day by day." 2 Corinthians 4:16

PERSONAL EVALUATION

Instead of asking you to reflect on discussion questions, I'd like to challenge you to go through the twelve steps of mental training. First do it on your own, then share your conclusions with another person. No one knows you like you do, which is why it is important to go through this on your own first. Be honest with yourself, then share your conclusions with either a teammate, the team, or your coach.

The LORD is my strength and my shield;
my heart trusts in him, and he helps me.
My heart leaps for joy,
and with my song I praise him. (Ps. 28:7)

—*Clark Marshall, #20, striker*

CHAPTER TEN

DEFINED IN BATTLE

"Whatever happens, conduct yourselves in
a manner worthy of the gospel of Christ. . . .
Stand firm in one spirit, contending as one man
for the faith of the gospel." —Philippians 1:27

"As water reflects a face, so one's life reflects
the heart." —Proverbs 27:19 (TNIV)

HEADLINES

- Your testimony is always on display.
- Adversity can define or break a team, depending how it is handled.
- Character is exposed when under fire.
- External responses reveal what is on the inside.
- Christian athletes are scrutinized and held to a higher standard.

COOLER HEADS WILL PREVAIL

Prior to our 2012 regional semifinal match, I called several coaches for a scouting report. Multiple coaches told me that if this particular team realized it would not be making the playoffs, it would do its best to ensure that some of our players were unable to play too.

By halftime we were winning 1–0. Up until that point, the game had been somewhat physical but not over the line. Coming out of halftime, we scored two goals in five minutes to take a 3–0 lead. Suddenly what the coaches had told me became a reality. For the next thirty-five minutes, the other team's players literally began trying to send our players to the hospital. When the players received yellow caution cards and were sent off the field, their coach greeted them with high fives and sent them back onto the field. As their players, coaches, and fans became more animated, I actually began to look around for security because I was not sure how the night would end. When all was said and done, the other team had accumulated seven yellow cards and two red cards (double yellow cards) in the span of thirty-five minutes. We had secured a 4–0 victory, but two of our players had sustained major injuries.

Throughout the entire match, I could not have been more proud of our boys. They had been swung at, thrown down, and called every name in the book. They had received cheap shots from behind, had their ankles swiped, and taken intentional elbows to the head. Yet they had not reacted or retaliated once. Their response was outstanding! The next morning, I was pleasantly surprised to receive emails from two of the officials from that match.

> I'd like to take this time to compliment you, your assistant and especially your boys' soccer team on your performance last night. As referees, these are games that we ask ourselves if we could have done anything different to prevent the utter disregard for you, your team and fans shown by the "the opposition" . . . the thing that stands out most to us [referees] is the professional way you, and especially your boys, handled the situation at hand. They never said anything to any of the

referee crew, accepted each call that may not have gone in their favor and moved on. It speaks well of you and your boys that they kept cool heads in the face of being the victims of playing a team that had seven cautions and two send offs . . . Again, thanks for your team's professional handling of a not so pleasant situation.

Last night was easily the most difficult match I have encountered in a long, long time. Nevertheless, it was truly a pleasure to officiate your side. Your team (and fans too for that matter) composed themselves with an amazing level of class and self-restraint. Your team was a real credit to your school regardless of the taunts from the stands to the contrary . . . We honestly could not have escaped that game without all of your understanding, cooperation and incredible professionalism.

I wish I could tell you that this is how all my teams and I have handled the tough situations we have encountered. Unfortunately, that is not the case. However, on that particular night, our guys handled themselves in a way that Paul describes as a "manner worthy of the gospel of Jesus Christ" (Phil. 1:27). Although we won more games as we pressed through playoffs, I was so proud to have walked off the field that evening knowing our players had represented Christ well. Christian teams often talk about playing for the glory of God. That night, I felt we certainly had done this and that God was pleased with our response.

THE TIPPING POINT

In every season comes the moment that I refer to as the "tipping point." A team can be either defined or broken as a result of a particular incident. There's no question of whether that moment will come to a team. The real question is how the team will handle the adversity when it does arrive. Under fire, true character is revealed, tested, and defined. Although such moments can be unnerving, any revelation is an outworking of who we are—although it may be played out in front of many other people. Who we are, *our being*, always precedes *our doing*, just as attitude always precedes the actions we take. It is never the other way around. If it were, then our worth and our value would be defined by our achievements. We don't want it to be this way! That would mean that we would stop being valuable as soon as we stopped performing.

Recently, I was coaching my son's club team. They had won the state cup in the fall and were now playing in the President's Cup Regional Tournament for a chance to go to the nationals in California. During a 4–1 victory over the South Carolina team, one of our team's forwards was fouled. When no call was made, he turned and lunged at the defender with both cleats up. He was red carded immediately and sent off for the remainder of the match and the one to follow.

Teams rise and fall based on how they react in such situations. Much was revealed about our team that weekend. We were winning our bracket and simply needed to win our next match to move on. However, the team unraveled before our eyes, and we ended up losing 2–1 to Texas the next morning and getting bumped from the tournament. What started out as a promising prospect abruptly ended on a sour note. Might we have had a different outcome with our leading scorer in the game? Maybe. However, we will never know.

TRUE CHARACTER EXPOSED

Such incidents are not uncommon. Professional sports give us many examples. Before reading through the following scenarios, I challenge you to read with eyes of discernment.

Ask yourself: What might have made each individual react in such a way? What does his or her reaction reveal about his or her character? How might I react or respond if placed in the same situation?

Be careful not to gloss over these issues and think you are above such behavior. Consider the thoughts that you have had toward the opposition when the heat gets turned up. Actions are one step removed from the thoughts that come into our minds. Be careful not to presume you are above behavior that you might find appalling at this moment. Peter gives us a warning in 1 Peter 5:8, "Be self-controlled and alert. Your enemy the devil prowls around like a roaring lion looking for someone to devour." Athletics is a great place for the Devil to go after Christians.

Scenario 1:

In a rematch fight between Evander Holyfield and Mike Tyson on June 28, 1997, Tyson bit a chunk out of Holyfield's ear and spit the one-inch piece of cartilage on the ring floor. As a result, the match ended, and Tyson and his boxing license were suspended.[1]

Scenario 2:

During the 2006 FIFA World Cup Final between France and Italy, the world watched as Frenchman Zinedine Zidane walked up to Marco Materazzi in the 110th minute and head-butted him in the chest, knocking him to the ground. Zidane was immediately ejected. The game ended up going to penalty kicks, and Zidane's team lost the PK shootout 5–3 to Italy. That was the final professional match of Zidane's career. Interestingly enough, France has immortalized the moment in the form of a bronze statue in the heart of the French capital. The action that left a nation heartbroken is appropriately named "Headbutt" and is referred to as "an ode to defeat."[2]

Scenario 3:

In 2004, then Indiana Pacer Ron Artest, now self-named Metta World Peace, became involved in the worst brawl in NBA history. He, along with teammate Stephen Jackson, charged into the stands and fought with fans during the final minute of their game against Detroit. Several people were injured, and a police investigation ensued. World Peace was suspended for eighty-six games and lost almost $5 million in salary for that year.[3]

Scenario 4:

University of New Mexico's (UNM) Elizabeth Lambert has been called the roughest soccer player in the world. In the many YouTube videos of a match between UNM and Brigham Young University on November 7, 2009, Lambert is seen punching players in the back, giving blows to their heads, and making late and dirty slide tackles. At one point she literally yanks a player to the ground by her ponytail, which became one of the most watched YouTube videos during the following week.[4] Despite such antics, her team lost the match, and she not only hurt her name but the reputation of women's soccer at UNM.

WATER INSIDE THE BOTTLE

Yes, these might be more over the top than normal examples of aggression, but in sports we see athletes lose their cool almost every day and do things that hurt both themselves and their teammates. A friend shared with me something he had heard author and speaker Paul Tripp say once during a speaking engagement, which illustrates this situation very well. He held up a water bottle and began to shake it. As he did, water spilled out onto the ground. When he asked the audience why water had spilled out of the bottle, someone replied that it had done so because he was shaking it.

While this is true, it was not the core answer. In reality, water spilled out of the bottle because water was in the bottle. Shaking the bottle only revealed what was inside. In the same manner, when life's circumstances cause us to blow up, we must not only look at the circumstance that caused us to react but look at our hearts and ask what needs to change. What part of your being is adversely affecting what you do on or off the field or court? In Zidane's case, Materazzi said something profane about either Zidane's mother or his sister. For World Peace, the tipping point came when someone in the stands threw a drink at him. In both of these cases, more than the profanity or thrown drink (the shaking of the bottle) caused them to get angry and react (the overflow of water). Their reactions revealed something deeper inside their hearts.

At times it does not take much for us to react to something. Have you ever stopped to ask yourself why you respond in a certain manner? Perhaps your life has been shaken so much that you erupt or explode. However, sometimes you start with an empty glass. Consider major events that can happen to you throughout a day. Maybe you are late to school, get a bad grade on a test, or are ignored by your boyfriend or girlfriend. Each event adds to your cup. After a while, your cup is so full that it begins to overflow. This is called *emotional flooding*. The smallest thing can cause your cup to overflow—and overflow it does. You have reacted, perhaps to the smallest thing, and there are now consequences to sort through.

This process is not uncommon. Know and identify it so that when your cup begins to fill, you can step away from the stress or avoid conflict that might not go so well at that moment. If you come to an athletic contest with your cup already over-flowing, speak with your coach. When this happens with my players, I treat them differently so as not to be the one who causes the waters to rise and their cups to spill over.

CALLED TO BE UNCOMMON

As Christians, we are called to be uncommon. We are called by God to be "set apart" (Rom. 1:1) and even to be a "peculiar people" (1 Peter 2:9 KJV). Jesus says, "Blessed are you when people insult you, persecute you and falsely say all kinds of evil against you because of me" (Matt. 5:11). When we bear the name of the Great King, plenty of people will look for us to stumble and fall. Many people want to point the finger at us and say, "You call yourself Christians."

No other sports figure today has been more scrutinized because of his profession of faith in Jesus Christ as his Lord and Savior than NFL quarterback Tim Tebow. When fellow NFL quarterback Jake Plummer suggested that he tone it down and not be so outspoken about his faith, Tebow responded by saying, "Anytime I get the opportunity to give the Lord some praise, He is due for it because of what He did for me and what he did . . . on the cross for all of us." He continued, "At the end of the day if all we're doing is winning and losing football games and scoring touchdowns, then we really haven't done a lot in our lives."[5]

Where does such conviction, courage, and confidence come from? I believe that Tim Tebow has been able to show such an unwavering commitment to the Lord in the face of adversity, criticism, and even ridicule because he believes in Hebrews 13:6: "The Lord is my helper; I will not be afraid. What can man do to me?" Tebow shows such consistency because he is living out of who he is (being). Think about it. If Tebow were living and responding out of what he *did*, consider how difficult that would be.

As a University of Florida quarterback, Tebow was touted as the best in the country, and he has a National Championship Trophy and a Heisman Trophy to prove it. He was drafted by the Denver Broncos to be the backup quarterback. After a 1–4 sluggish start to the 2011 Bronco season, Tebow was given an opportunity to be the starting quarterback. He never looked back. At one point he led the Broncos to six consecutive wins. Most of these were very dramatic, as over and over Tebow drove down the field in overtime or with time expiring to bring the Broncos another memorable win. These performances were only outdone by his record-breaking 29–23 win over the mighty Pittsburgh Steelers in overtime. In this game he not only endeared himself to the Bronco fans but to many people across the nation, breaking record after record when he threw for 316 yards on ten completions.

After a season of relentless harassment from critics about his throwing ability and quarterback style, Tebow appeared to have not only silenced the critics but solidified his job as the quarterback of the Denver Broncos for years to come. However, in the off-season, the Indianapolis Colts released superstar quarterback Peyton Manning, and in a surprising turn of events, the Denver Bronco ownership decided to put their future in his hands. Without a doubt, Manning is one of the best quarterbacks of all time. However, what would this mean for Tebow, and how would he respond? On March 21, 2012, *USA Today* reported that Tebow said, "I understand what the Broncos are going through and what they're dealing with . . . not many times do you have an opportunity to get a player like Peyton Manning."[6] Before long Tebow was traded to the New York Jets who already had a competent quarterback in Mark Sanchez. Regarding this trade, Tebow said, "Looking forward to seeing him soon and working with him. Definitely have a lot of respect for him. . . . He is such a classy guy and handles himself so well." He continued by saying he would "come in and compete and get better as a quarterback and find other areas to help the team . . . and that's my goal . . . I always try to put the team first."[7]

In a couple of years, Tebow has gone from perennial college quarterback to backup NFL quarterback to starting, highly successful, and highly criticized quarterback to being traded, then being relegated to the bench and finally cut from the New York Jets. This roller-coaster experience has not shaken Tebow's commitment or his resolve to work, train, and live his life in a way that brings honor to the name of Christ. Proverbs 27:19 says, "As water reflects the face, so one's life reflects the heart" (TNIV).

Tebow is human. In the quietness of his heart, he is alone. There may be times when the pressures, the critics, and the relentless high expectations must be close to overwhelming. However, through all the highs and lows he has experienced as a quarterback, he has clearly shown millions and millions of spectators around the world what is on the inside. Tim Tebow has battled, been tested, and is respected for consistency under fire. For Tebow, the circumstances have not defined the man. Instead the man has shaped the circumstances by living from the inside out! Thank you, Tim—we need more examples like you to show us how God designed us to live!

PERSONAL EVALUATION/DISCUSSION QUESTIONS

1. Have you personally been at the "tipping point" or had your "cup overflow" in a game? If yes, how did you respond? What was the result?

2. Have you seen another team member get to the "tipping point" and cross the line? Recall the incident. What happened as a result? How did the rest of the team respond?

3. If you had the opportunity for a "redo," what might you do differently both personally and if you were to see a teammate cross the line?

4. When your life gets shaken up in athletics, what spills out? Do you see patterns, reactions, first impulses, sudden spikes in emotion? What do these responses tell you about who you are and who you are becoming? If you don't like what you see, what changes need to take place?

5. Though not perfect, Tim Tebow has given us an excellent example to follow. How has his life served as a motivation for you in how to battle from the inside out in your sport?

STAGE 3

PLAYOFFS

"When we started winning championships, there was an understanding among all twelve players about what our roles were. We knew our responsibilities and we knew our capabilities. Those were the kinds of thing we had to understand and accept if we were going to win championships."[1]

—*Michael Jordan*

"There are plenty of teams in every sport that have great players and never win titles. Most of the time, those players aren't willing to sacrifice for the greater good of the team. The funny thing is, in the end, their unwillingness to sacrifice only makes individual goals more difficult to achieve. One thing I believe to the fullest is that if you think and achieve as a team, the individual accolades will take care of themselves. Talent wins games but teamwork and intelligence wins championships!"[2]

—*Michael Jordan*

Better is a poor person who walks in his integrity
than one who is crooked in speech and is a fool.
(Prov. 19:1 ESV)

—*Taylor Black, #11, center midfielder*

CHAPTER ELEVEN

COLLECTIVE SEPARATION

*"I appeal to you, brothers, in the name of our
Lord Jesus Christ, that all of you agree with one
another so that there may be no divisions among
you and that you may be perfectly united in mind
and thought." —1 Corinthians 1:10*

HEADLINES

- Excellence begins with you!
- Separation from competition must be predetermined.
- Championship teams have a "closer" mind-set.

AFTER WAITING for forty-three years, the National Hockey
League (NHL) Los Angeles Kings won their first Stanley Cup
on June 11, 2012 by decisively defeating the New Jersey Devils
with a 6–1 score! The next morning an article titled "Kings
Pulled Together at the Right Time" caught my eye. As I read
about this team, I came across a related article, "Kings Owe
Cup Run to Tight Group." I was particularly struck by forward
Dustin Penner's comments. He said, "You see it with every
team, they go through slumps. . . . There's a point where we
could have quit. We could have said, maybe next year, but we

don't have those types of people in our organization, in our locker room."[1]

NOT FOR EVERYONE

Playoffs and championships are not for every team. The good teams make playoffs, the great teams compete for championship titles, and the exceptional teams raise the trophy and championship banner. To win championships, something must happen inside each player and to the team as a whole. Although the change is intangible, sometimes it feels as though you can almost physically touch it. If you get this, you will feel it in the depths of you who are.

The reality is that no matter the sport, when the field of teams is narrowed, the competition level becomes so intense and the margin becomes so small that something has to give. Nothing can be simply business as usual. Excellence is not an accident! Excellence requires change, and it must begin one player at a time . . . and must spread through the team like wildfire! If it spreads through the entire team, it is amazing what can happen, even when a team with less talent is matched against a more skilled team. So . . . what is it?

SEPARATION TIME

As playoffs near, it is not uncommon for my players to hear me say, "Men, it is time to separate!" This does not imply that we have been lazing around or not striving for success up to this point. For several months, the team has been working to come together. After all, every team's goal is for the team to peak at just the right time. Everyone talks about this goal, but not everyone achieves it! It's not as easy or natural as you might think.

To get to the place where a team can peak, much must happen along the way. Players must know the rules of engagement and how they ought to conduct themselves (chapter four); they must get to know their teammates well (chapter five); they must engage and own the vision, direction, and possibilities of the team (chapters six and seven); they must work at communicating with each other and with the coaches (chapter eight); and they must play and train and battle from the inside out to be mentally rugged (chapter ten). By this point, the team has the potential to click on all levels. Issues that have caused the team to falter or that inhibited forward progression should have been put behind the team long ago. The team should have gone through the storming phase and not around it. With norms established, the team should be performing well.

Unfortunately, I have not been able to say this of some of my teams for various reasons. Sometimes there is a lack of chemistry between the players. Sometimes the players lack an internal voice that coaches them on the field and at practice. Sometimes players lack the desire and willingness to sell out and pay the price. Sometimes the cause is my lack of ability to lead the team and understand what my players need at a given moment. For a host of reasons, teams often get stuck and can't press to the performing stage of team development.

However, some teams appear to be clawing the ground and breathing fire from their nostrils, ready to take the entire experience to the next level. When I say we need to separate, they know what I mean: no matter what the competition is doing to prepare, we will prepare better, work harder, be stronger, train with more desire and determination and vigor than anyone else, and we will do it together. If you play a team sport, there is no other way!

Separation as a Team

In 2008 the Boston Celtics, coached by Glenn "Doc" Rivers, defeated the L.A. Lakers in game six to win their seventeenth

NBA championship. During that season, they had adopted a word, *ubuntu*, to define them as a team. This South African word indicates unity and interconnectedness and literally means "we are who we are through others."[2] Do you get a sense of how tightly connected and interwoven the players had to be to embody this word? Three superstars—Kevin Garnett, Ray Allen, and Paul Pierce—had converged to wear the Celtic green. Living out *ubuntu* meant that these three men had to be willing to defer to one another, take fewer shots, make fewer individual points, and share both the ball and the spotlight. All three quickly proved they were more than willing to do this. They realized that the sum was greater than the parts! At that point, none of them had an NBA championship ring. They all had led the league at some point in individual scoring, assists, or rebounds, but that was not what they were after! In the end, they separated as a team from the rest of the NBA and claimed another title to hang in the rafters.

Separation as an Individual

You might be thinking, "This all sounds good, but what am I to do? What is my role?" This matter first must be settled by you and addressed within you. Coaches cannot give you your role once the game begins. At a U.S. Soccer Federation soccer clinic I attended some years ago, former U.S. Soccer National Team Coach Bruce Arena told all the coaches in the room, "Coaches, remember that when the game begins, you are worth only about 10 percent." The field is our classroom. It is primarily where instruction takes place. However, once the game begins, the players are the ones who make the major difference. So what is your role? Simply put . . . great players must be willing to pay the price, sell out, outwork everyone, run to challenges, embrace good hard work, and examine themselves to see if they can do anything to personally prepare themselves and their team for the playoff push.

PREDETERMINE THE SEASON OUTCOME

Getting to the top is grueling. Sacrifices must be made. You cannot wait until you are in the battle to decide to separate. You must determine this in advance. I like the passage in the Bible where Daniel, in Babylonian captivity, had a choice either to eat the king's choice meats or to hold to his Jewish customs and beliefs. "But Daniel purposed in his heart that he would not defile himself with the portion of the king's delicacies" (Dan. 1:8 NKJV). The key word here is "purposed." He had made up his mind before temptation was placed in front of him.

There are a myriad of things that tempt you, as an athlete, not to offer your best, and come game day there is little to nothing you can do about it. Consider the food, or fuel, you put in your body, the discipline to get sleep and cut other non-essentials out of daily living(such as TV, gaming, and so on), how you train when no one is looking, and even how you do life with friends. For example, the stress you bring into a game will determine your performance. Stress causes fatigue, is distracting, and causes reactions when they often are not warranted. These things cannot be taken lightly if you expect to play at peak performance.

Separating means you are willing to do little things that others are not willing to do. If you don't think that will make a difference, ask yourself when you last lost a game by one point, fell six inches short of the goal line, were beaten by less than a second, dropped a pass, missed an open layup, missed a penalty kick or an extra point, failed to get the ball over the net, dropped a ball that should have been a catch, had the puck or ball clang off the crossbar, or were beaten in a photo finish at the finish line. The list could go on and on.

Little things make a huge difference. I know this extremely well. As I have already stated, probably what stands out most in my coaching career is the fact that I have lost *two* state championships on penalty kicks. While I never took one of the kicks myself, I have asked myself what I could have done to better prepare my players for those season-ending moments.

THE CLOSER

Sports Illustrated ran an article in its June 25, 2012 issue titled "The Icemen Cometh." The article set up the last couple of games of the NBA championship finals between the Miami Heat and the Oklahoma City Thunder. The caption under the title read "As the Heat seized an early lead over the Thunder, one thing became clear: The title will go to the team whose star can best close out a game."[3]

Since the 1970s, the *closer* is the guy in baseball who usually comes in during the final inning to protect the lead and slam the door on the other team's thoughts of making a comeback. The term *closer* came to the NBA a few years ago "as a way to sort out the superstars into smaller categories. . . . Kobe Bryant, who had won five championships, was the closer. James, who has wilted in the playoffs was not the closer"[4] . . . until 2012! The writer of the article, Lee Jenkins, said, "The difference between a closer and a choker, in this age of overreaction, can be one misguided fadeaway."[5]

An article in a later issue of *Sports Illustrated* discussed LeBron James and his promise to bring a title to Miami. Before Miami Heat's 2012 championship season, Dwyane Wade had been the leader of the team. However, at one point in the season Wade told James, "I need you to lead this team now."[6] Even during games he would say to James, "I need you to lead us right now."[7] By the time playoffs began, roles were defined. Wade said that it was personally hard for him to do that but "it was easy for him to do it for the team."[8] History speaks for itself: James was spectacular in the 2012 season and on multiple occasions proved he could be a closer.

Hall of Fame guard Sam Jones won ten championships in twelve seasons with the Boston Celtics and was 9–0 in game seven of a seven-game series. He said, "At the end Coach [Red] Auerbach would call a play for me, and I would make the shot."[9] Jenkins wrote, "The best closers have always been the best players (see Michael Jordan), but the best players have not always been the best closers."[10] The closer is most comfortable when others are rattled. " 'It's supposed to be quietest in the eye of the tornado,' [Reggie] Miller says. 'That's how it was for me.' "[11] The closer demands the ball for his team's sake as much as his own. "There's a certain selfishness involved, but it's not selfish," says William Parham, a sports psychologist who has worked with NBA players. "The closer has an uncompromising belief in his ability."[12]

However, no matter the sport, the other players on the team must understand the situation, their surroundings, and what is expected of them. "Champions close as a group," Jenkins writes. "Durant depends on a screener and a passer, and a screener for the passer. James needs a screener, a cutter and shooters to space the floor."[13]

Are you getting the idea here? Everyone is important, everyone is required, and everyone must understand the situation at hand! The team must *collectively* embrace this idea, and when players see a team member not pressing in the same direction, they must address the situation right away in order to get back on track as quickly as possible. There is no time for detours. In this case, peer pressure can be very useful in driving the team forward.

I will never forget when I saw this firsthand during my first year of coaching. We had won the district championship and were looking to make a deep run at the state title. To do so, we held an extra Saturday practice to get ready for the regional championship match against St. Johns in Jacksonville, Florida. A sophomore player started to mess around, distracting the team from our primary focus. Ben, our senior goalkeeper, stepped up and addressed the situation before I had a chance to say something. He quickly walked over to the guy, grabbed him by his jersey, and said, with his eyes blazing, "Hey, I'm going to state with or without you. You have to decide if you're on board or not. We don't have time to mess around right now, so make your decision. Are you in or out?"

Whoa! Ben had said everything and more that I wanted to say; however, he was probably way more successful than I ever could have been in that situation. The other player wisely and very quickly said, "Sorry, Ben, I'm in!" The practice was more focused and more deliberate for the remainder of the session.

Ben got it! Ben understood his role as a senior goal-keeper and captain. He had that closer mentality. In the game against St. John, we ended up going to a shootout. With the shootout score at 4–4, we needed Ben to make a stop! As the shot was taken, Ben dove to his left and made a spectacular save. However, the referee gave the player another chance, saying Ben had moved early. With no time to get discouraged, frustrated, or rattled, to argue, or even to hesitate, Ben yelled to me as I was standing at half-field, "Don't worry, coach! I got this one too!" As promised, Ben managed to make another amazing save! A freshman went on to score the decisive penalty kick and send our exuberant team to the state finals.

Ben handled not only the penalty-kick contest but also led the team in practice on the Saturday before. I tie the two events tightly together, because for Ben, "closing" began long before the end of the game. He had been mentally preparing for that moment for some time. Looking back on that season,

I believe that Ben's leadership was more instrumental to our 1993 State Championship than I ever realized at the time!

HYSTERICAL STRENGTH

Rhiannon Hull was a distance runner who trained ferociously. She was a two-time state champ in the 4 x 400 meter and she twice competed at the NCAA championship at the University of Oregon in cross-country. After graduating from Oregon she married and had two children, and she and her husband decided to relocate from California to Costa Rica. Rhiannon and her six-year-old son Julian moved, and her husband Norm would follow in two months. However, everything changed one day when the two of them were playing in the ocean and suddenly, 130 feet offshore, they got caught in the riptide. It was described as "half an hour in a head-on battle against an enemy of prodigious power, while Rhiannon strained to save 45 pounds of the most precious cargo imaginable. Julian would later describe what he was doing as 'standing on Mommy.' "[14]

Apparently Rhiannon had been able to shoulder press her son while treading water long enough for surfers to finally reach them. As the surfer grabbed Julian, Rhiannon slipped into the sea, breathing her last breath. How was she able to do what she did for such an extended period of time? After all, she was only 5'2" and 100 pounds of sinewy muscle, which did not prove to be an asset on this particular day.

As a group of South African scientists wrote,

"An unusual feature of humans is their ability to produce extraordinary feats of strength (hysterical strength) or inconceivable performances of endurance when the only alternative is to face death." These superhero exploits, the scientists concluded, are the result of the human brain forcing the body to keep much of its muscle power in reserve unless the power is required to preserve life. . . . Our brain ensures that we can never perform our best until the stakes are dire. [15]

Recently scientists have also concluded that since the brain stingily withholds a physical reserve, a mental finish line is required to make a heavy stamina withdrawal from the body. In order to go the hardest, our brain needs to know when and where we are going to stop.[16] Many studies have been done to prove this fact. For example, if a distance runner or cyclist knows where the finish line is, they will withdraw extraordinary power to push through that line. However, if you were to move or suddenly extend that line at the point they crossed the original finish line, their energy and effort would plummet. In such cases, the brain has expended to the body a high output of strength, but when the finish line moves, the brain and the body cannot recalibrate. For Rhiannan, as a distance runner she had programmed her mind to summon and expend all the physical and mental energy possible to reach the threshold of exhaustion just to the moment of her son being saved. Once he was released to safety, she had nothing to left to save herself as she had now crossed over her ultimate finish line with the goal being to see her son saved.

While this is certainly a dramatic story, there is application for us. While I am in no way suggesting you push yourself to death, what I am saying is that very few people train, play, and live in a way that taps into the mental capacity within, which will offer physical energy beyond where they originally thought they could go. Too many of us establish our own "finish lines" that severely limit our performance. What might happen if individuals on a team collectively decided that the finish line needed to move farther away, then decided to go and pursue that finish line with all the mental and physical fortitude they could muster? Now that would be a group of individuals and a team I would love to watch!

THE PERFECT EXAMPLE

But isn't this what we are challenged in Scripture to do? Look at this passage from Hebrews 12:1: "Therefore, since we are surrounded by such a great cloud of witnesses, let us throw off everything that hinders and the sin that so easily entangles, and let us run with perseverance the race marked out for us." If we are playing for the glory of God and using the talents he has entrusted to us, then the *we* and the *us* in this passage are directed at us and *for* us! So, athletes, compete with perseverance, knowing that the "witnesses" have gone before us, setting an example for how to run the race and run hard to the end! Is that not a cool part of this passage?

I am not asking you to enter uncharted waters or unfamiliar territory. This is not like going out on a trail run on an overgrown path without any markers to provide direction. No! I am challenging you to run down the path that was forged by Christ himself! The next verse speaks of Christ as the "author and perfecter of our faith"! Christ didn't run one leg of the race. Instead he ran the entire race ahead of us despite the worst conditions. "For the joy set before him [he] endured the cross, scorning its shame, and sat down at the right hand of the throne of God" (Heb. 12:2).

Now is not the time to compete in the way Paul describes in 1 Corinthians 9:26: running aimlessly or boxing the air. Instead, be on purpose! "Let your eyes look straight ahead, fix your gaze directly before you" (Prov. 4:25).

Doesn't Scripture just come alive? You might not have ever thought there could be such a parallel between athletics and the Christian faith. I would be remiss to end here, though. Athletics merely give us a glimpse of the rest of life as applicable lessons are learned and applied. Step out of the playing arena and consider these passages of Scripture on the greatest "race" ever run—a race of eternal consequence. Remember, athletics are great, but they are a microcosm of the real thing.

PERSONAL EVALUATION/DISCUSSION QUESTIONS

1. How would you describe your current or past team's post-season preparation and conclusion? How about your own preparation?

2. Thinking about your last season, if you could to do it over again, what might you personally do differently? What effect might this change or changes have had on the rest of the team?

3. Does your team have a "closer" who is so mentally tough that the team looks to him or her for guidance and direction? If so, and if it is not you, how might you encourage that person in his or her role? (Everyone needs encouragement. Supporting the closer is a great service to the team!)

4. How did the story of Rhiannon personally challenge you? Discuss how you have viewed "finish lines."

5. How does Hebrews 12:1–2 speak to your heart? What is God saying to you? What role might he be asking you to fill? Are you up for the challenge, knowing that you do not run alone? Discuss.

6. How are you running the Christian race? Do you need to throw off certain things that are slowing you down? If yes, identify them and ask others (close friend, coach, etc.) to provide accountability.

> I can do all things through Christ which strengtheneth me.
> (Phil. 4:13 KJV)
>
> —*Gene Nelson, assistant coach*

CHAPTER TWELVE

STAYING ON CENTER

"Therefore I do not run like a man running
aimlessly; I do not fight like a man beating the
air. No, I beat my body and make it my slave so
that after I have preached to others, I myself will
not be disqualified for the prize."
—*1 Corinthians 9:26–27*

HEADLINES

- Don't compromise your beliefs and principles in pursuit of winning.
- Focus on how you run the race instead of the final outcome.

VERY FEW, IF ANY, serious athletes would say their desire is simply to compete and that the outcome does not matter. In fact, many might say that if we are not keeping score, why even play the game? Without a doubt, winning is a blast. There is nothing like holding a championship trophy over your head. The feeling of satisfaction, of completeness, and of knowing that only one team could be the champion and that it was your team is priceless! Unless you experience this for yourself, it is difficult to describe.

However, once you win, and win big, your natural inclination is to want more. So what will you do to secure another victory? To what lengths will you go to be the best? What are you willing to pay for the thrill of a championship? These questions may seem natural to ask, yet the practical answers can be very destructive, as was discovered with the New Orleans Saints during the spring of 2012.

PAY TO INJURE PROGRAM

During the 2009 NFL season, Saints Defensive Coordinator Gregg Williams would stand in front of his players with envelopes filled with cash. Each envelope had certain bonus amounts in it. For example, a defender could get $1,500 for knocking a player out of a game or $1,000 for a "cart-off" when a player had to be helped off the field. *Sports Illustrated* reported that middle linebacker and defensive captain Jonathan Vilma had personally offered a $10,000 bounty to any player who knocked Minnesota Vikings quarterback Brett Favre out of the game during the 2010 NFC Championship game. Coach Williams was often heard to say, "Kill the head and the body will die!"[1] If the quarterback could be taken from the game, the rest of the team might fall. The Saints not only defeated the Vikings in overtime 31–28, but two weeks later they defeated the Indianapolis Colts 31–17 in Super Bowl XLIV.[2]

So what were the consequences for such behavior? *Sports Illustrated* reported:

> The coordinator of the Saints' defense and the bounty system, Gregg Williams, is suspended from the NFL indefinitely, head coach Sean Payton is suspended for one year, general manager Mickey Loomis is suspended for the first eight games of the season and assistant defensive coach Joe Vitt is suspended for the first six games of the season. In addition, the Saints were fined $500,000.[3]

Jonathan Vilma was suspended for the entire season and several teammates also received partial season suspensions.[4]

CHEAT TO WIN

Sports Illustrated recently ran an interesting cover story on the issue of using performance-enhancing drugs in sports. While the article profiles players who "juiced" or took steroids and those who resisted, most talked of the intense pressure to be a user. The article included a question written in big black letters, the essence of what many baseball players feel: "The line between the minors and the majors can be so thin. What would you do to cross that line, even for a day?"[5]

The article profiles various professional baseball players, concluding with former MLB pitcher Dan Naulty, who admitted to using steroids. He spent the money he had earned in playing baseball to pay for therapy and counseling.[6] Today he is a new man in Christ and is a pastor of Rock Community Church in Yorba Linda, California. On the day the reporter attended his church, Naulty was preaching on Colossians 3:2: "Set your minds on things above, not on earthly things." Although his life has changed for the better, the cost has been great, and he and his family have paid a dear price.

CENTER YOURSELF

Stories on the New Orleans Saints' pay-to-injure bounty program, the steroid usage among athletes, and other compromising actions reveal the by-product of not staying on center. When pursuing the almighty win and looking for an advantage, non-Christians and Christians alike are susceptible to temptations to cut corners, make compromises, or run after quick fixes. In a playoff run, with everything on the line, it is easy to forget what you stand for and believe in. Much of how you respond results from your character and the outworking of who you are.

Below are several key points to assist in keeping you and your team on center.

My identity and worth is found in Christ, not in my accomplishments. In Romans 8:15–16, Paul says we are no longer slaves but sons and daughters. Does that not change everything? A son or a daughter has no reason to fear. You can freely do your best, knowing that you are God's beloved child and that he will love you no less if your team does not win and no more if it does. If God's love is unconditional, we can perform as well as we can without the pressure that might drive us to compromise what we know is right. As a dad, I can say that my love for my own sons has never changed based on how many goals they scored in a game.

How I run the race is more important than the outcome. This is a hard truth to handle and not an overly popular message. In our outcome-driven world with pressure placed on us in every direction, we are made to believe that only outcomes matter. In 1 Corinthians 9:24, Paul says, "Do you not know that in a race all the runners run, but only one gets the prize? Run in such a way as to get the prize." If we stopped there, the message would be grossly incomplete. Paul continues, "Everyone who competes in the games goes into strict training. They do it to get a crown that will not last; but we do it to get a crown that will last forever" (v. 25). Now the picture becomes clearer. Strict training has less to with physical training and more to do with bringing our actions into alignment with who we are as sons and daughters of the Great King! If there is one area where we must not compromise, this is it!

I must stay true to my vision. In chapter six, I asked you several important questions. If you took those questions seriously, you now have answers ready for review. The questions were: *Where are we going? How are we going to get there?* and *What is my role?* Review your answer to each of these questions. This vision was developed during a time in the season when you were fresh and excited and the emotions of playoffs were not a factor! Pay special attention to the question *How are we going to get there?* As an individual and even as a team, ask whether you have stayed true to the course of accomplishing your goals and followed the process to get there.

Adjust, refocus, and commit to staying on center! Your team may come up with a phrase or a few words that are unique to the team for a specific time. In my first year of coaching, we adopted the phrase "Just one more game!" after a devotions session. In part, the focus was to not look past the next game in front of us. But the bigger picture was actually taken from the story about Samson. He had been shackled between two huge pillars that supported a building where three thousand Philistines were gathered, the same people who had gouged out his eyes. At that moment, Samson prayed this prayer to God, "O Sovereign LORD, remember me. O God, please strengthen me just once more, and let me with one blow get revenge on the Philistines for my two eyes" (Judg. 16:28). That year we recognized that like Samson we are powerless to do anything good on our own strength and need to call on the Lord to give us the necessary strength, regardless of the outcome, to do our very best for his honor and glory.

For our 2012 season, we had a pre-game chant using the Latin words, "Soli Deo gloria!" Interpreted, these words mean "only to the glory of God." We will often talk that through with each other, evaluating our own hearts and exhorting one another to stay on center.

PERSONAL EVALUATION/DISCUSSION QUESTIONS

1. What does being and staying on center mean to you personally?

2. In your attitudes or actions, where have you drifted off center? How can you refocus?

3. Some of you might disagree with my point that how you run the race is more important than the outcome. However, what might the outcome look like, or how might you feel, if you give no thought or concern to how you run the race? What might transpire?

4. What adjustments do your team and you personally need to consider to stay on center or return to being on center?

May I never boast except in the cross of our Lord Jesus Christ, through which the world has been crucified to me, and I to the world. (Gal. 6:14)

— *Richard Reinink, #14, center back*

CHAPTER THIRTEEN

VICTORY IN DEFEAT

"Therefore, my dear brothers, stand firm.
Let nothing move you. Always give yourselves
fully to the work of the Lord, because you know
that your labor in the Lord is not in vain."
—*1 Corinthians 15:58*

HEADLINES

- Teams often overlook preparing how to lose well.
- A team can be successful in defeat.
- Players must conduct individual assessments of their performances and attitudes following a defeat.
- Personal evaluation and reflection will prepare players for future games.

As the final seconds ticked away, spectators watched as our 2012 varsity men's soccer team seniors—many of whom had played on the team for the past four years—concluded their season with a loss. Although it's always difficult to end on a loss, in reality almost everyone wraps up his or her season this way. The NFL Championship, the World Series, the Stanley Cup Finals, the soccer World Cup, the NBA Finals, the U.S.

161

Open, the Masters, and every other league championship will see only one team finish on top. The rest will conclude on a losing note. Isn't it interesting that we spend so much time talking about winning and what we must do to win when so few teams actually end their season with a win? While no one really likes to talk about losing, and it never is something that you plan to do, it is something that you should be prepared for. Before getting too far ahead of ourselves, we should define and put into context several key words such as *losing* and *failure*.

Losing does not always mean failure. We see all the time that great teams can dominate play for the majority of a match and then still lose. On August 15, 2012, the United States National Soccer Team was playing Mexico in Mexico. It had *never* won a match against Mexico on Mexican soil. After being dominated for the strong majority of the match, the US went up 1-0 with only 10 minutes left to play. It was clear to everyone watching that the better team was Mexico, and yet the match just did not go their way.[1] Mexico lost that match, and yet it does not necessarily mean that they failed. True, they failed to secure the win, but they were very successful in how they attacked and defended. In a future game, such play will serve them well.

Conversely, there is a big difference between losing and getting beaten. If you lose, something went wrong. Typically a loss happens as a result of faulty tactics, sheer laziness, or just too many mistakes and errors.[2] Unfortunately your opponent may not so much win the game as you lose the game. If you have been part of one of these games you know what I am talking about. They sting for a while because you know the outcome should have been different.

On the other hand, getting beaten is a different story. Usually if you are beaten, it is because your opponent was bigger, faster, and stronger; they outplayed you, outworked you, outperformed you, had more mental focus and concentration, and as a result were able to capitalize on your weaknesses. In short, they earned and deserved and you did not.[3] Losing and getting beaten are both hard to swallow, but losing is by far the worse of the two.

BY THE NUMBERS

Over the course of four years, our 2012 men's soccer team had seventy-three wins, thirteen losses, and six ties. They had scored 345 goals and surrendered sixty-three. Of their seventy-three wins, fifty-five had been shutouts. They had three district championships, three regional championships, four sectional championships to get to state, one state-runner up, and one state championship. They had certainly made their mark, and it seemed only fitting that this group should conclude with a win!

Prior to their senior season, the twelve seniors on the team knew that the pressure was on them. In 2010 they had lost the state championship game in penalty kicks, and in 2011 they had won the state championship 2–0. It was not uncommon for the boys to hear the expectations other people had for them, assuming that the only way they could end the season well would be with another state championship.

AN HONORABLE LOSS

As our 2012 season was winding down, we had as tough a road to win state as any team. Going into playoffs, we were ranked number three in the state. Our top district opponent was ranked number four, and the team we would have to beat to get to state was ranked number two. As the playoffs progressed, we found ourselves staring at an elimination game against this number-two ranked team that had won its last seventeen games in a row. In a thrilling game, we won 2–1 in overtime,

163

earning a spot in the eight-team state tournament. We simply needed to wait and see who we would be playing. In Tennessee, a blind draw determines the tournament bracket. Some might compare it to the college football Bowl Championship Series (BCS) bowls arrangements. My team, now the second highest ranked team in the state tournament, was drawn to play against the number one team in the state. I believe both sides knew that this was really the state championship match.

As the game wore on, it became clear that it would be a barnstormer! After concluding regulation 0–0, both sides made desperate attempts to get the decisive goal. Our opponents found the break they were looking for as a ball was deflected off one of our players on a free kick and redirected into our goal. Even in the concluding seconds of the game, our guys refused to quit. However, when the last whistle sounded, it was clear that this group of young men would end their four-year high school soccer career on a loss . . . at least, that was what the scoreboard said.

Although the opposition went on to win the state tournament as we suspected it would, I did not view our game as the end but actually the beginning. As we huddled together on the field one last time, I looked into my players' eyes and told them how proud I was of them. First, I told them that they had played the best game of the season. It had been their fourth overtime game in thirteen days. They were exhausted. They had left everything on the field. I was so incredibly proud of how they had reached into the depths of their being to secure the go-ahead goal and to defend their own net with great veracity. The sting of defeat hurt, and there was a sense of deep sadness in losing our seniors to the next thing that the Lord was calling them to in life. However, I told them that they should not feel a sense of incompleteness for the season. I told them that they had come into the soccer program many years ago as boys and now were leaving as men. Although a scoreboard said we were finished, these guys were just beginning the journey to a very bright future.

TRUE MEASURE OF SUCCESS

John Wooden speaks of two principles that his father taught him as a boy. He told him to 1) not try to be better than someone else and 2) always try to be the best he could be. Wooden said,

> Dad reasoned that whether we were better than someone else should not be the focus because our position in relation to others was out of our control. . . . We could not control another's performance, nor could we control how we would be ranked. All we could do was our best . . . and let the results take care of themselves.[4]

Too often we get so focused on the other team or individual across from us that we lose sight of what we can control—ourselves. I could not have been more proud of my 2012 team. Although a defeat can sting badly, it is much worse when you know in the quietness of your own heart—when no one is around, and it is only you and the Lord—that you could have done more but instead held back from offering your best. The night after we lost a game, I did not have an empty pit in my stomach as if we had let one slip away that we should have won. The game could have gone either way. Two heavyweights had stepped into a ring that night and slugged it out for 110 minutes. Without a doubt, by Wooden's definition, my guys were incredibly successful that evening! So how should we look at this differently, maybe even to the point where we can declare a victory in defeat?

Consider the following statements. Following a loss, look yourself in the mirror and, as honestly and as transparently

165

as possible, determine whether or not you are able to declare these following statements of yourself.

I trained and prepared for this match the best I possibly could. A great example of this is found in late Tiaina "Junior" Seau who played professional football for the San Diego Chargers and the New England Patriots. Commenting on Seau, fellow teammate Rodney Harrison said,

> One day . . . I asked him why he practiced so hard. . . . He said, "Rodney, I get paid to practice. I play the games for free." He said anybody can go out in front of 70,000 people and get excited and play a game, but it takes a special person to practice at game speed. That changed my whole career, and my life. When I retired from the Patriots, coach (Bill) Belichick said I practiced harder than any player he had in 30 years of coaching. That was because of Junior.[5]

I did not carry fear or worry with me into the game. Any negative thinking triggers negative emotions and fuels more negative thinking. When you don't soon experience the results that you were hoping for, it becomes easy to get scared and imagine a loss instead of a victory. This negative self-talk can become a self-fulfilling prophecy. Think of a player who looks across the field or court and says, "There is no way I can beat that person." Making such statements either out loud or in your head is a sure way to get a good old-fashioned "beat down"—not at the hands of the opposition but because you dealt it to yourself. The opposition is typically tough enough. There is no sense in battling yourself as well.

I played the best game I could play. This is not to say that you played a perfect game. Rather, you should have played at the highest caliber you could. As guys on our team will say, "Don't bring the weak sauce tonight!" In other words, bring nothing less than your best to the game.

I recognize what I need to work on to improve my game. One of the greatest teachers in any sport is a loss. A loss can accomplish more than an exceptional coach with a great game plan because a loss often reveals weaknesses, deficiencies, and other areas that need to be addressed. If you take time to evaluate your game and where you might improve, your loss can be a very, very valuable tool.

I have not assigned blame or guilt to another teammate. When a game is on the line, there are times when your own team manages to defeat itself. Unfortunately, at moments like these, we look for scapegoats. We want to say, "It is your fault" or "if you had just done X, Y, or Z differently, we would have been fine." This type of response has no place on a team. I am always saying that we rise and fall together as a team. This motto ensures that we do not take undue credit as individuals, and it also protects individuals from taking the brunt of a loss.

In April 1993 during the NCAA men's basketball finals, the North Carolina Tar Heels were winning by two points with seconds remaining in the game. Chris Webber, a University of Michigan player, was in the corner of the court in front of his bench and suddenly called a timeout. Unfortunately, his team did not have any timeouts remaining. As a result, Michigan was hit with a technical, and North Carolina made the free throw. Michigan ended up losing the championship.[6] How devastating! What do you say in such moments? Few people pointed out that Webber's own teammates on the bench were screaming for him to call the timeout. When you are part of a team, you must rise and fall *together*—don't ever sell out a teammate . . . or a coach!

There are things I did do well in the contest that I must continue. Notice where I put this comment. I did not put it right after you asked if you played the best game. Self-improvement and lack of blame for others must come first because they require humility, self-analysis, and an evaluation not only of your effort (doing) but also your attitude (being).

If you are able to work through these six points after a match—and I mean really wrestle with them and learn through them—then I believe it is entirely possible that the defeats you suffer may prove to be some of the best teaching moments in your life. You just need to recognize them for that and not miss the moment!

I will never forget the last game of regular season in 2000. We were playing Tampa Prep in Florida. It was their senior night. Our boys looked at it as just another match and a final tune-up before going into playoffs. I am not sure how Tampa Prep viewed the match. However, as the game ensued, it became clear that we were in for a long night. When the final whistle blew, I was handed the worst loss of my coaching career . . . to this day. We lost 0–7!

The crazy thing is that the other team took ten shots and not one of them was inside the eighteen-yard box. It was as though they had guided missiles that found every corner of our net. After the fourth amazing goal, I turned to my assistant coach and said, "I don't believe God intends for us to win this game!" I vividly remember our conversation as we sat around talking about it with our team afterward. One guy said, "What the heck just happened?" Without hesitating, another guy said, "I'm not sure, but we better figure it out really quick!"

Today, I look at that game as one of the best games I have ever been part of. The self- and team-evaluation that took place afterward was remarkable. By the time we were done and ready to head back to Orlando, we were a different team! Looking back, I firmly believe that game was the defining moment in our team's season and the catalyst that helped us to win the 2000 State Championship!

Scottish journalist B. C. Forbes, founder of *Forbes Magazine*, once said, "History has demonstrated that the most notable winners usually encountered heartbreaking obstacles before they triumphed. They won because they refused to become discouraged by their defeats."[7]

What about you? Unless you are a member of some freakishly phenomenal team that never loses, you will experience many losses during your playing days. Just like with winning, losing is not the main thing. What is most important is how you deal with that loss. Keep a big perspective on future games and how you might transfer the lessons you have learned to life outside athletics.

As I mentioned in chapter seven, life will deal you setbacks and difficulties—you can count on that. The question is what you will do as a response over the next few minutes, days, and weeks ahead.

PERSONAL EVALUATION/DISCUSSION QUESTIONS

1. Prior to reading this chapter, how would you process a loss?

2. How do John Wooden's words on defining success help to shape your opinion of a defeat? How do his words redirect your focus and thoughts before and after a contest?

3. Of the six areas for post-game (loss) evaluation, which do you believe you currently do well already?

4. Of these six areas, which do you believe will take the most work to address? Why? How do you intend to ensure that you address this area?

5. Write out a definition that reflects your opinion of what defeat in a contest actually is.

Come to me, all you who are weary and burdened, and I will give you rest. Take my yoke upon you and learn from me, for I am gentle and humble in heart, and you will find rest for your souls. For my yoke is easy and my burden is light. (Matt. 11:28–30)

—*Michael Powell, #3, forward*

CHAPTER FOURTEEN

THE ARMS AROUND US

*"A friend loves at all times, and a brother
is born for adversity." —Proverbs 17:17*

HEADLINES

- Identifying your bent toward either tasks or relationships will shape your team's experience.
- Knowing and being known by your teammates is rewarding and beneficial to the team's overall success.
- Relationships through athletics should transcend the game itself.

A SURPRISING PHONE CALL

Twenty-three years ago, God caused two men's paths to cross in a very unlikely manner. I was a college soccer player, and Jim Arnold was a college basketball player. We both ended up in the same campus house our freshmen year. I was a Christian, and at the time he was not. However, we did have a few things in common. We were both athletes, and we both liked to keep a neat room. When it was time to go to sleep, we wanted it quiet. In our sophomore year, we decided to room together. For the most part, that was a good arrangement. However, Jim left at the conclusion of that year. During his time away, the Lord took hold of Jim's heart and drew him to himself.

Back home in Virginia, Jim married and had a young son but was no longer in college. One day he received a call from a man he had known in high school. The guy was some years younger but had always looked up to Jim's playing ability as a point guard. He called to see if Jim wanted to finish his college education and his playing days at Bryan College.

You might not think that this seems like a big deal. However, when John Stonestreet called Jim, he was not a college recruiter, or merely a college student, or even just a basketball player on the team. No, he was the senior starting point guard for Bryan College. When he made that call, he knew that if Jim accepted his invitation, he would take almost every one of his minutes since he was the better point guard. Sure enough, that is exactly what happened. Jim became the starting point guard while John spent his senior season watching from the bench. Jim was great at running the point and during his senior year, he was second in the nation, all divisions, in assists per game!

You might be thinking, "Why in the world would someone make such a call? Who in his right mind would essentially say goodbye to his senior season?" Honestly, very few would do something like that. However, John Stonestreet was an uncommon man and a true teammate. He recognized that for his team to be even more successful, it needed Jim to run the point. What a noble act!

While you might find John's actions shocking, you might also wonder where you can find teammates like that. Instead of looking for that teammate, ask yourself what you need to do to be that teammate. By focusing and working on yourself, you just might make a difference in the life of someone else. You might not be able to accomplish what Jim did, but you could do what John did. What a difference that might make! It made a big difference for Jim and his family . . . and for the rest of the Bryan College's basketball team.

TASK OR RELATIONSHIPS

One of the mistakes I sometimes make as a coach is to focus on tasks instead of relationships. Over the years I have worked to find the balance between being goal oriented and outcome focused while at the same time enjoying the journey with my players and taking the time to not just know about them but to really know them for who they are.

Each of us naturally falls somewhere on the task/relationship continuum. Where are you? Where are you most naturally drawn? While everyone is different, few people are perfectly balanced in their task/relationship orientation. Most are drawn to one perspective over the other. Maybe the following statements will help to reveal your position in this matter. As you read through the following statements, give each one a number between 1 and 5, with 1 being least important and 5 being most important.

Task Oriented:
- My individual statistics are important to me.
- I am willing to invest long hours to improve my skills as a player.
- Where the team finishes in playoffs is important to me.
- On trips to away games, I spend the time focusing and preparing for the contest.
- My relational time with my teammates is primarily focused on practices and games.

Relationship Oriented:
- Team accomplishments are most important to me.
- I enjoy playing my sport primarily because of the people I do it with.
- More than winning games, I hope to develop strong lasting relationships with my teammates.
- On trips to away games, I spend the time talking with my teammates.
- My relational time with my teammates extends beyond the time spent in practices and games.

As you work through these statements, what do your responses say about you? Typically extremes are not good. Do you find that you are too strongly oriented to one perspective over the other? While this is not meant to be used for scientific conclusion, it is my hope that you can catch a glimpse of your personal tendencies in regard to task/relationship orientation. Note where things might be out of balance so that you can take steps to remedy them.

For the sake of this chapter and topic, I want you to focus on the relational side of being an athlete. Throughout this book, we have spent a great deal of time talking about outcomes, tasks, being goal oriented, and pursuing team vision. However, if we are not involved in relationships, something is radically missing! We are meant to spend our lives in community with others. The verse at the start of this chapter captures what it means to be a good teammate and to engage in the lives of one another. There will be many times throughout a season when you will need other individuals or your whole team in order to survive those moments of adversity. These moments can come to us on or off the field. However, if you have chosen not to engage and develop relationships with your teammates, you will be deprived of necessary friendships that will hold you up in moments of difficulty.

Without fail, life deals us blows that we can only pull through alongside others. Over the years my players have dealt with parents going through divorce, the deaths of parents, suspension from school, difficult interpersonal relationships with others outside the team (often dating relationships), struggles with sin in their lives, etc. If you are honest with yourself, you will realize that there are certain things in your own life right now that you would love to share with another person.

We naturally want to share ourselves with others and be with others. God said of Adam, "It is not good for the man to be alone" (Gen. 2:18). This does not mean that we need others simply to be in proximity to us, but we need others to walk with us through inevitable life struggles. These moments are often too difficult to navigate without the support, encouragement, and exhortation of friends. You spend an enormous amount of time with the teammates you train and play alongside. Do you know them? Do they know you?

TO BE KNOWN

What does it really mean to be known? I believe every human being cries out to be known and loved. King David asked God, "Search me, O God, and know my heart" (Ps. 139:23). Does it get any more real than that? For David to ask the King of the Universe to look deep into his inmost being and to know him speaks to a longing we all have! Being part of an athletic team opens up the possibility of being truly known and loved by a group of people—your teammates.

Consider the following questions as you evaluate your personal situation.

- Do your teammates know of interests you have other than your sport? (Whenever I find out something about my players, it allows me to engage with them and get to know them in a completely different way.)

- Have you ever told your teammates your personal goals, desires, passions, and ambitions following high school or college?
- Have you ever invited your teammates to your home?
- Have you ever let your teammates see your heart, as David asked God to see his, confessing struggles, hidden sins, or heartbreaks that are still open wounds?
- Have you opened God's Word together to study what he might reveal for your lives?
- Are you willing to allow teammates to be the "iron sharpening iron" in your life (Prov. 27:17)?

If you have struggled to answer these statements in the affirmative, I would challenge you to consider opening yourself in a way that will enrich not only your life and the life of your teammates but also change the team dynamics off and on the field.

If you find yourself struggling to affirm many or any of these statements, it may be that you just have never really thought about this much before. However, it might be that there is something more startling in play. If your desire is not really to let others into your life or know you well, in reality you deprive yourself from knowing yourself more fully. In our desire to be left alone, we simply become more and more deceived as to who we really are. If we don't allow others to hold up the mirror to our lives and invite them to point out our blind spots that distort who we can be, we are only hurting ourselves. The idea of the independent, self-made person is actually counter-scriptural. Hebrews 3:12-13 says,

See to it, brothers, that none of you has a sinful, unbelieving heart that turns away from the living God. *But*

176

encourage one another daily, as long as it is called Today, so that none of you may be hardened by sin's deceitfulness.

We need each other daily. Mutual accountability and openness to each other's lives is not only rewarding, but necessary.

A MAN DOWN

When teammates work through difficult life situations and open themselves up to be truly known by each other, it transforms how they play together. They now play for more than a win or a specific game; they play for each other and alongside each other. Life suddenly becomes much more meaningful and greater than simply playing a game. As I noted in the introduction of this book, I challenged my players not to make our state championship game about the game but about their relationships.

One of the most moving examples I saw of this was when we were playing a team from Nashville called Christ Presbyterian Academy (CPA) in our 2012 spring season. As the game began, I noticed that they were playing down a man and only had ten players on the field. Less than a minute into the game, one of their players stepped to the half-field line to check into the game. Not knowing what was going on, I asked, "Did you guys not know you were playing a man down?"

The answer was surprising and moving. He said, "We knew, sir. You see, last year one of our players suddenly died, and we are not the same without him. So we decided to start every game a man down to honor him."

This team got it! The players understood that there is more to athletics than training and playing in a contest. Their relationships and the events in their lives literally changed how they prepared for and played each game. They were essentially saying that the relationship they had had with this player was so important to them that it was as if he were on the field with them.

The apostle John wrote, "There is no fear in love. But perfect love drives out fear" (1 John 4:18). Yes, there will be some risk in this. Letting someone into your life is risky every time you do it. It means offering that person something deeply personal and deeply meaningful—your own self. However, take heart. The benefits outweigh the risks. If you offer your arms to support other teammates and are willing to be held up by them, your athletic team experience will be unparalleled. However, if you keep them folded and will not accept or offer them to others, it will be difficult for you to be a true teammate.

Remember my roommate Jim Arnold? While we have never played on the same team, we have shared experiences, stories, and a great deal of each other's lives for the past twenty-three years. I am currently the head of the upper school at Chattanooga Christian School, where he serves as my assistant upper school head. We have worked side by side for fifteen years. The friendship we developed many years ago has grown, and I know my life is better for having been around him. Due to the nature of our friendship and our work, we have had heated discussions many times, as he sharpens me and I press back . . . and vice versa. However, I can honestly say that in our fifteen years of working together, I have never closed a day feeling upset with him. Our friendship always trumps whatever issue we are dealing with at a particular time. I need him in my life, and I believe there are times I offer him mutual support and sharpening.

There will always be issues to debate and difficult circumstances to wrestle with. However, like changing seasons, these come and go. When you have a good friend and teammate, differences just don't seem quite as big because you focus more on what you have in common than not. It's not too late to keep your sport from merely being about a game. Make it about people. Make it about your teammates! You will forever be glad that you did. Games come and go, but relationships are eternal!

PERSONAL EVALUATION/DISCUSSION QUESTIONS

1. How would you summarize your current task/relationship orientation? Does something need to change? If yes, what might it be?

2. Does anyone on your team really know you? Describe that relationship. If your answer is no, why might that be?

3. How might your team dynamics change if your focus on relationships changed?

4. What do you wish someone on your team knew about you? Who might you talk to about this?

> Jabez cried out to the God of Israel, "Oh, that you would bless me and enlarge my territory! Let your hand be with me, and keep me from harm so that I will be free from pain." And God granted his request. (1 Chron. 4:10)
>
> —*Rocklin Shumaker, #2, striker*

CHAPTER FIFTEEN

CHAMPIONSHIPS

"Now thanks be unto God, which always causeth
us to triumph in Christ, and maketh manifest
the savour of his knowledge by us in every place."
—*2 Corinthians 2:14 (KJV)*

HEADLINES

- Be humble in victory and deflect praise to others.
- Championships are to be enjoyed, but the game does not mark the end.
- Championships provide new opportunities—seize them!

THE GREEN BAY PACKERS, THE Boston Celtics, the New York Yankees, and the North Carolina Tar Heels women's soccer team all have one thing in common: each team has won championship after championship and separated itself from the competition. These teams are either loved or hated because of their ability to win championships!

Up to this point, this book has been preparing and guiding you through all the stages of your team's season, from preseason, through the regular season, to playoffs, and now to the final match of a season: the championship!

By God's grace, I have led four teams to state championship victories. Regardless of the level, championships are not just the end of a great season. They are an open door for new opportunities!

For most, a championship win is their end goal: the pinnacle and the shining moment of a season. Without a doubt, winning a championship is an excellent accomplishment. But then what? Is athletics all about the gold medal draped around your neck or the trophy hoisted over your head? I would argue that drawing this conclusion would be very shortsighted. After a championship is attained, there is still much to accomplish!

GIVE CREDIT WHERE CREDIT IS DUE

The very first thing to do is to thank the Giver of "every good and perfect gift" (James 1:17). Many professional players unapologetically acknowledge Christ. The world took note when Tim Tebow knelt in recognition of God's goodness to him. In 2 Corinthians 2:14, Paul says, "Now thanks be unto God, which always causeth us to triumph in Christ, and maketh manifest the savour of his knowledge by us in every place" (KJV). This wonderful verse captures the essence of what I am communicating. There are several important points in it: God leads us, God gives us the victory, and God allows us the opportunity to point others to Christ. In other words, when people watch you play, whether you win or lose, you should handle the entire event—from pre-game, to game time, to post-game—in a manner that diffuses the aroma of Christ, drawing people to you so that you can point them to Christ. This is what the psalmist is getting at when he writes, "Not to us, LORD, not to us but to your name be the glory, because of your love and faithfulness" (Ps. 115:1).

WINNING DOES NOT EQUAL SUPERIORITY

In order to embrace the above statement, you must be humble. Jesus said, "For all those who exalt themselves will be humbled, and those who humble themselves will be exalted" (Luke 14:11). I also commonly refer to the proverb quoted by James: "God opposes the proud but shows favor to the humble" (James 4:6). Scripture says that if God is for us, who can be against us? In the same way, if God is against us, it does not matter who is for us. We can't oppose God and expect to come out the victor!

During the 2012 NFL post-season, in reference to Tebow's strong faith in God, Terrell Suggs of the Baltimore Ravens was quoted as saying, "With all due respect, we don't need God on our sidelines!"[1] The Ravens had a chance to see Tebow's team, the Denver Broncos, in playoffs. All they needed to do was beat the New England Patriots. However, they lost by a field goal and got to watch the Broncos defeat the Pittsburgh Steelers. One sports writer commented, "Though Suggs undoubtedly was joking, certain topics entail slightly more risk than others. Though God may not be working to help a team win, it wouldn't be wise to invite Him to help a team lose."[2]

CONSIDER YOUR RESPONSE

No matter what level you are playing at, if you win a championship, eyes are on you. When the final whistle blows, people listen to how you respond. The words you say can end up on the news that evening or in the paper the next morning. After LeBron James won his first NBA title with the Miami Heat, his first public response was to swear, as millions of people around the world listened in. That was disappointing. When you are a champion, commend the other team, elevate your teammates, be gracious and thankful when people compliment you or your team, and remember to choose your words wisely, as they will certainly be remembered.

After 16-year-old Gabby Douglas became the first African-American woman ever to win the gold medal in the Women's Gymnastics All-Around, she said, "It is everything I thought it would be; being the Olympic champion, it definitely is an amazing feeling. And I give all the glory to God. It's kind of a win-win situation. The glory goes up to Him and the blessings fall down on me," Douglas testified in the interview.[3] Later she also took to social networking site Twitter to continue her praise. She tweeted: "Let all that I am praise the LORD; may I never forget the good things He does for me."[4]

During the Olympics, Gabby Douglas was the most clicked athlete on NBCOlympics.com. She attracted 18.27 million views to the website. This was more than double the amount that visited the site to see Michael Phelps.[5] At the young age of 16, Gabby knew there were many eyes upon her and that to choose her actions and words carefully were very important!

SAVOR THE MOMENT

I remember sitting at breakfast the morning of our 2000 state championship game. We had won the year before, and the players sitting at the breakfast table in our hotel were already throwing around the word "three-peat." Surprised, I told them that we needed to secure the victory that evening before we could even begin to think about next year.

In 2011, on the way back from the state championship title victory match, players on the bus started asking me about summer fitness training schedules and who we would be getting on the schedule for next year. I had to challenge them to simply enjoy and savor the moment. I vividly remember saying to some of the 2011 players, "Guys, it's been only one hour since we won the championship. I appreciate your enthusiasm;

however, you need to stop and take in this moment. Enjoy it with your team, because it will pass quickly."

Unfortunately, we are a society and a generation that is constantly thinking about what will come next. Back in college, my soccer team would take low impact backpacking trips, meaning we carried all our gear in *and* out and made as small an impact on nature as possible. Coach would take all our watches so we would not worry about the next moment. How often each day do you check to see the time, to see who has emailed you or posted something on Facebook or tweeted a message? I can tell you that when you don't have these things at your immediate disposal, you are freed to simply enjoy the moment you are in!

If you have won a championship, you are a champion until someone takes the title from you. Typically, that leaves you one full year. Enjoy and savor that moment. You have accomplished something that few teams ever experience!

THE TROPHY DOES NOT DEFINE YOU!

Every sport has great players who are haunted by the fact that they never won a championship. Basketball greats such as Charles Barkley and Karl Malone never won an NBA championship and are consequently defined as having fallen short. The Buffalo Bills are an example of a whole team that has come close to earning a championship, yet after four tries has not yet achieved one Super Bowl victory.

What about those players and teams that have won championships? Are their lives more complete? Have they *arrived*? While a championship is a wonderful accomplishment, remember that it is something that you *did* and not *who you are*. This is a hard truth to embrace but one worthy of strong consideration. Be careful not to find your life's purpose and fulfillment in winning a championship. If that is where you find validation, then a loss or a failure to earn another championship has the

185

potential to rob you of your sense of identity, worth, or value. The championship is just a bonus, an added benefit of the hard, diligent, and dedicated work you did throughout your journey. In this case, there was something extra special at the end of the journey—just don't let it define you.

TAKE INVENTORY . . .

Taking inventory is necessary for returning players. Just because you won a championship does not mean you do not have lessons to learn and areas of growth to address. Sometimes, for a variety of reasons, teams and players do not play their best game in championships. Looking back, I believe two of our semifinal matches to get to the championship were better played than the championship itself. Some struggle with nerves, some play not to lose, and almost all have areas where they can improve. Success tends to distort your view of reality and gloss over your shortcomings. The journey is more important than the outcome, so even after a championship, take an inventory and assess how you might sharpen yourself. Jot down notes while it is still fresh in your mind. In time, all you will remember is the trophy and the championship medal.

RECOGNIZE THE EYE ON YOU . . . AND THE X ON YOUR BACK

As you look toward next season, know that players are coming in behind you and watching you very intently. What will they learn? What will they pick up? What will they do and become as a consequence of being around you? I can say from experience that it is brutally hard to win championships back to back. When you are an underdog, you play free, knowing that you have everything to gain and nothing to lose. When you are on top, you have everything to lose and nothing to gain. Even if you win another championship, you have maintained your place and not advanced.

The season following one of our championships, players from a rival team told our players that their coach had gathered them for a team meeting to hand out their schedule. When they received their schedule, the only team listed on the whole paper was our team. I took this as a compliment that of all the teams they could schedule, they decided to only play us. What an honor!

Kidding aside, recognize that every time you take the field, it is an opportunity for your opponents to measure themselves. By winning a championship, you become the "measuring stick" by which other teams judge their abilities.

The very first game of our 2012 season, following our 2011 championship, we played a district opponent and tied them 1–1. We outshot them 22–3 but just could not find the back of the net. After the game, a couple of their players came up to me and said, "Well, coach, I guess we will see you in state, huh?" A little taken aback by such a bold prediction for both teams, I replied, "I'm not able to comment on you all, but my team has a lot of work to do before we can even begin to think of state." We were their measuring stick, and in their estimation, they measured up and were contenders.

In his book, Tim Tebow talks of having to deal with this tension following the Florida Gaters' 2006 BCS Championship. His team had "earned an incredible platform from which to influence kids and others for good," he writes. "It was something that I believe we should take seriously and build upon. A lot of my teammates agreed and came ready to go."[6] However, he bemoans the fact that too many of the guys came into the season with a sense of entitlement and with expectations that positions were theirs and were simply going to be handed back to them. He said the sense of commitment and hard work that had helped them to earn the national championship title simply was not there. He also noted that some of the new players were excited about being part of Florida history but had not yet come to terms with the fact that "this history was earned off the sweat and sacrifice of others—not by them."[7]

Recognize that if you are blessed to be part of a championship season, the culmination of that time does not lie in the trophy or medal that you have been given but rather in the life lessons that you have learned, applied, and lived out. Remembering this will benefit you far beyond your days as an athlete.

PERSONAL EVALUATION/DISCUSSION QUESTIONS

1. Share examples (positive or negative) of how you have seen teams handle championships. Note the circumstances that caused positive or negative responses.

2. It has been said that "failing to plan is planning to fail." If you have not won a championship, I encourage you to consider how you might respond if you should win one. Which of the key points in this chapter would come most naturally and which would be more difficult? Why? Explain your answers.

3. If you have won a championship, which of these key points have you successfully pursued and accomplished? If you had a chance for a "redo," what might you do differently?

4. While each of the key points in this chapter is important, have each of your teammates rank them in order of importance. Compare notes and defend your position based on what you believe is most important. If you are blessed with a championship, make sure that you do not neglect to follow through and live them out!

STAGE 4

POST-SEASON

"There is a choice you have to make,
in everything you do.
So keep in mind that in the end,
the choice you make, makes you." [1]

—*John Wooden*

For God so loved the world that he gave his one and only Son, that whoever believes in him shall not perish but have eternal life. (John 3:16)

—*Taylor Farrar, #6, defensive midfielder*

CHAPTER SIXTEEN

FOR LIFE

*"Whatever you have learned or received or heard
from me, or seen in me—put it into practice.
And the God of peace will be with you."*
—*Philippians 4:9*

HEADLINES

- To what end have you played athletics?
- Lessons learned through athletics must transfer to life.
- There are no timeouts just because the season is over. Redeem the time!

ON JUNE, 4, 2012, *Sports Illustrated* magazine ran an article titled "Last Stand of the Big Three," in reference to the Celtics' three point shooting specialist Ray Allen and defensive specialists Kevin Garnett and Paul Pierce. The article asked if they had one more run in them to win a championship. (In the end, they fell short in the Eastern Conference Championship in the final game of a best of seven series.) The article closes with these words: "The end is near. 'I literally won't allow myself to go down that road,' says [Coach Doc] Rivers. 'Whenever that day comes, that will be an emotional day.' And yet the certainty of that sad day is to be treasured, because it brings out the best in those who play every game as if it may be their last."[1]

There is a saying that "all good things must come to an end." But I am not so sure that saying is entirely true. It is true that you cannot continue to play high school, college, or professional athletics forever. However, if your final game—even if it is a championship—is the culmination of everything you've learned, what does this say about what you were striving for? Was it all about the game? Was that your sole focus? Spend a few minutes reflecting on

- the first time you went to practice as a youngster,
- the number of games and practices you have trained and prepared for,
- the teammates with whom you have played over the years,
- the things you have chosen *not* to do so that you could participate in athletics.

You have made a serious investment over the years. If "time is money" and you consider the amount of time invested, all the hours spent alongside teammates preparing, training, and playing have made you a wealthy person.

IT'S NOT OVER 'TIL IT'S OVER!

One of the most thrilling games I have ever coached was when we were down 0–1 during the 1999 state championship match. With minutes remaining, we began to push players forward to create goal scoring opportunities. Simultaneously, the other team began driving balls off the sidelines in what appeared to be a tactic to use up the remaining time. With seven seconds left, we had a throw-in on the defending team's side of the field. What resulted could not have been scripted better. The ball never hit the ground as two of our players' heads flicked the ball on and one player hit a full volley shot that slammed the ball into the back of the net for the equalizer. We had a 1–1 score with only three seconds of regulation time remaining. When overtime came, we found the back of the net once again, securing a thrilling, come-from-behind state championship! That night every player learned the valuable lesson that a game is never, never over until the final whistle blows.

But even the final whistle does not signal the end. Thinking that it does compartmentalizes athletics from the rest of life. Athletics cannot be put into a small box, only to be pulled out every now and then so you can rummage through trophies, plaques, certificates, medals, newspaper clippings, and video coverage of your team in action. This would only be looking *back*, nostalgically thinking about the "good ol' days" as great days gone by forever.

I firmly believe that your athletic experience is not over! I would be deeply saddened to learn that players left our soccer program and closed the book, so to speak, on that time in their lives. I am not proposing that we should not move forward in life, but I am challenging you to consider how your athletic experiences and lessons are transferrable to the life beyond them.

If my players say I, their coach, taught them little that extends beyond the soccer field, then I have grossly wasted their time and talents by having them chase after a black and white soccer ball. (When I put it in those terms, it sounds rather silly, doesn't it?) A transcendent cause must lie behind your training and competition. Lessons learned, or possibly lessons missed, can be applied to your life even when your playing days are through.

So when is it over? I would say it is never over!

FRIENDS FOR LIFE

In my book *We Became Men,* I dedicate an entire chapter to friendship. It is so important to have friends who stand beside us in moments of great joy and moments of great pain, friends who love us like Jonathan loved David as they wept together and embraced as true brothers. I never want to minimize the great sacrifices made by our American soldiers, by making a hasty comparison but for most people, the closest they will ever come to a battlefield will be the athletic arena. Few other places in life make evident such deep commitments, loyalty, sacrifice, and dependence on others. When the final whistle blows and the final game has been played, why must these relationships draw to a close as well? They should not! They will look different, and the amount of time you have to invest in them will change, but I hope you will treasure these relationships.

I regret that there are some relationships I have not kept up with over the years. Even though they were deeply meaningful to me, I did not prioritize maintaining them. Don't make the same mistake. Hold on to them; draw on them. You will be glad you did! Granted, your friendships will never be the same, as circumstances and events change; however, relationships can endure! Since you are brothers or sisters in the Lord, don't neglect relationships that can continue through to eternity.

THE FIELD IS OUR CLASSROOM

I am intrigued by the educational debate about where to place athletics in schools. Are they "extracurricular" or are they "cocurricular?" In my opinion, they are cocurricular. They are part of the teaching and learning process. If students are to be taught in the classroom in a way that prepares them for life after high school or college, then we should approach athletics or their cocurricular activities in such a manner. In *We Became Men*, I often mention things I learned from my college coach. He prepared me and my teammates to compete in games, but more important than that, he prepared us for the "game of life." I am eternally grateful for his influence.

What did you learn in what may have been the longest "class" you ever took? What lessons were you taught from a young age that stayed constant even though your coaches may have changed? What transcendent truths must you hold to and apply to your life? I hope my own players will take the following skills and qualities with them wherever they go and whatever they do: commitment, dedication, perseverance, conflict resolution, problem solving, risk taking, leadership, followership, time management, encouragement, handling of praise and criticism, submission to authority, enjoying the moment, finding the positives in everything, working hard, being ethical, performing for an audience of One, and relying on others.

The lessons taught and learned in athletics are transferrable in some way to every area of life. When I consider what I am doing and the opportunity I have to influence others, I see myself less as a soccer coach and more as a life coach. As a player, this might be one of the most transferrable "classroom" experiences you have. Take notes, listen, and learn. Many years from now, you will be glad you did!

WHAT DIFFERENCE DOES IT ALL MAKE?

It makes all the difference in the world! I am saddened to the core when I see one of my players deliberately choose to lead a life that is not in accord with the real "Coach"—our Lord and Savior, Jesus Christ! Jesus said, "From everyone who has been given much, much will be demanded; and from the one who has been entrusted with much, much more will be asked" (Luke 12:48). I urge you to not squander what has been entrusted to you by your coaches and your teammates.

Granted, your coaches have said or done things that you do not want to emulate. It is good to note these as well. At times I have lost sleep over occasions when I led my team poorly. These too are great classroom experiences. Don't look at such circumstances as an excuse to grow bitter or resentful. Please recognize the source. Your coaches are not the standard. Sometimes coaches will point you in the right direction, and other times they may fail in this area. Extend grace where possible, but also use this as a means to grow personally.

There is a point where you have to own your faith journey. Lessons learned through athletics are great tools to bring you further down this path.

THERE ARE NO TIMEOUTS!

The time following high school graduation or the end of your college career can be as rocky a road as you have ever seen. I hate to watch players flounder, make poor decisions, and generally struggle during these years. It seems almost as if someone has said, "You can call a timeout whenever you want, and you are the official who can restart the clock whenever you want." This is not the case! There are no timeouts, you are not the official, and the clock *is* running. So what will you do with the time that you have been given? Paul told the Ephesians to make "the most of every opportunity, because the days are evil" (Eph. 5:16). He told the Corinthians,

> Do you not know that your bodies are temples of the Holy Spirit, who is in you, whom you have received from God? You are not your own; you were bought at a price. Therefore honor God with your bodies. (1 Cor. 6:19–20)

When we borrow something from someone, we want to return it to him or her in the best shape possible. Should this not also be the case with our bodies and our lives? Paul pointed out that because Jesus bought us with his blood, we should honor God with our bodies. What does that mean for how we live? Paul says,

> Live as children of light (for the fruit of the light consists in all goodness, righteousness and truth) and find out what pleases the Lord. Have nothing to do with the fruitless deeds of darkness, but rather expose them. It is shameful even to mention what the disobedient do in secret. But everything exposed by the light becomes visible—and everything that is illuminated becomes a light. This is why it is said:

> "Wake up, sleeper,
>   rise from the dead,
> and Christ will shine on you."

A NOTE FROM COACH

As this book draws to a close, consider some words from the apostle Paul. To any athlete that has played for me in the past, I offer you these words. Though not mine, they are as heartfelt as though they were penned by me, written for you! Walk in them! (If you have not played for me, know I am already praying for those who will read this book and asking God that you will be blessed in so doing.)

> I thank my God every time I remember you. In all my prayers for all of you, I always pray with joy because of your partnership in the gospel from the first day until now, being confident of this, that *he who began a good work in you will carry it on to completion until the day of Christ Jesus.*

197

It is right for me to feel this way about all of you, since I have you in my heart and, whether I am in chains or defending and confirming the gospel, all of you share in God's grace with me. God can testify how I long for all of you with the affection of Christ Jesus.

And this is my prayer: that your love may abound more and more in knowledge and depth of insight, so that you may be able to discern what is best and may be pure and blameless for the day of Christ, filled with the fruit of righteousness that comes through Jesus Christ—to the glory and praise of God. (Phil.1:3–11)

PERSONAL EVALUATION/DISCUSSION QUESTIONS

1. How much time have you invested in athletics over the years? Can you quantify this?

2. During your time playing athletics, what are the top 3–4 things you have learned that you believe are transferrable to life off the court or field?

3. What are those areas where you currently struggle or might struggle that would require an unofficial "timeout?" What accountability might you summon from your friends, mentors, or coaches to help you walk through the next phase of your life?

4. Looking ahead, how might you redeem the time or make the most of every opportunity following the time you graduate from high school and through your college years? What will keep you on track so you do not swerve to the left or to the right?

Let your eyes look straight ahead;
    fix your gaze directly before you.
Give careful thought to the paths for your feet
    and be steadfast in all your ways.
Do not turn to the right or the left;
    keep your foot from evil.
My son [or daughter], pay attention to my wisdom,
    turn your ear to my words of insight,
that you may maintain discretion
    and your lips may preserve knowledge.
(Prov. 4: 25–27, 5:1–2)

STAGE 5

LEADERSHIP DEVELOPMENT

"Aim to be a leader and you will be disappointed,
for very few people wish to be led. Aim to be a servant,
and you will never be without a job."

—*Anonymous*

Rejoice always, pray without ceasing, give thanks in all circumstances; for this is the will of God in Christ Jesus for you. (1 Thess. 5:16–18 ESV)

—*Roy Anderson, #4, center back*

CHAPTER SEVENTEEN

CAPTAINS' CLUB

*"And let us consider how we may spur
one another on toward love and good deeds,
not giving up meeting together, as some are
in the habit of doing, but encouraging one
another—and all the more as you see the Day
approaching." —Hebrews 10:24–25*

HEADLINES

- Captains are invaluable to the success of a team!
- Assumptions of players' leadership abilities are often made when selecting captains.
- Leadership can be learned.
- A Captains' Club will develop leaders, and everyone will benefit.

THE POSITION OF a team captain is vital to the success of the team. Captains are coaches on the field or court and are the coach's voice to carry the coach's philosophy and to execute the coach's game plan. However, players and coaches alike often make errors when extending the title to certain players or when electing the captain as a team.

The primary area of concern is that players too often do not receive leadership training. Just calling someone captain does not make him or her a leader. In the same way, just being a senior does not make someone a leader. I have seen sophomores more fit and qualified to lead than many seniors.

Although people can possess some inner qualities that serve them well as team leaders, thankfully leadership can be learned. We often hear people say a person is a "natural born leader." I do not entirely agree with this statement. If this were the case, the thousands and thousands of books written on leadership would be a waste of time to write and a waste of money to purchase—and also pointless to read. Rather, leadership can and must be taught in order to be properly learned. A safe practice ground must be extended to leaders-in-training, since they will make mistakes and need to know mistakes are OK. However, such parameters and opportunities are rarely discussed and established.

Tension and frustration can often mount between coaches and captains because of a lack of understanding of roles and expectations and a subpar job of providing leadership training for team captains. Coaches assume a captain knows what he or she should do, and a captain expects the coach to teach him or her how to lead and to explain the boundaries and parameters of this new role. Far too often, the training and the explaining never happen . . . at least to the necessary level. The results of this confusing arrangement are unsettling at best. I am reminded of David's words to the Lord:

> Show me your ways, Lord,
>   teach me your paths;
> guide me in your truth and teach me,
>   for you are God my Savior,
>   and my hope is in you all day long. (Ps. 25:4–5)

Imagine that is the posture of a coach before the Lord and, to a lesser extent, of players before their coach. The king of Israel humbly acknowledged that he could not and did not know what to do without the help and guidance of the Lord. It is not only OK, but it is necessary for you as a player to first admit that you don't know exactly how to lead and to ask for assistance from your coach. Go to your coach, like King David did to the Lord, and say, "Coach, would you please show me, teach me, and guide me?" A humble acknowledgment that you need to be taught about leadership so that you best lead will start your coach-captain relationship on a good foot and should set up honest and transparent dialogue between you and your coach.

Personally, I have failed many captains over the years. I have seen some qualities in certain athletes that, if developed, would have served certain captains very well and complemented my role as coach. Unfortunately, I failed to ensure that this leadership development happened. This was a costly and unfortunate mistake that I do not wish to repeat.

To aid not only our captains and coaches, but the entire athletic program, we recently started a new initiative at our school called the Captains' Club. This is designed to offer leadership training for all the captains of the various athletic teams within our school. In addition, underclassmen who show a desire to take steps of leadership are also invited to attend. What we have found is that in selecting and involving underclassmen, the captains and coaches experience more traction with owning and implementing team development concepts within the culture and existing dynamics of the team.

We offer this club in the fall, winter, and spring for three months at a time. The purpose of the Captains' Club is to draw the athletic leadership of the various seasonal sports together on a weekly basis to:

- train leaders,
- support coaches,
- unify teams and
- represent our "Head Coach," Jesus Christ.

In 1 Corinthians 12:12, Paul talks about the body of Christ as one body with many members, which each have various functions. In a similar manner, each school has one team unified under its team name, yet it has many members with different functions that are played out in the various teams.

I lead the captains in a twenty-minute presentation and discussion focused on a particular leadership topic. Then I extend an opportunity for individual team breakout sessions where leaders (captains and "understudies") can analyze and implement what we discussed within their team, as is applicable. Coaches are often present and either observe or engage with their team leaders in these discussions. The club builds outstanding shared leadership, understanding, and appreciation of captains and coaches within a specific sport and across the various seasonal sports.

We keep five desired outcomes in front of us to ensure we stay on target:

- To consistently apply leadership to how our athletes compete,
- To help different members of the body (teams) to support each other and to work as one,
- To support coaches as they build and develop their team and its leaders,

- To turn our athletic department into a venue where leaders are trained and empowered to lead in their sport and beyond, and
- To lead our athletes to represent Christ well "whether in plenty or in want" (Phil. 4:12).

We meet Monday morning at 7 a.m. for forty-five minutes. This has proved to be a rich time for the student athletes and their coaches. I would highly encourage student athletes to discuss this with their coaches and/or their school athletic directors.

I firmly believe that leadership development can transform your team and the overall athletic culture at your school. While you might never be a captain, the influence of the leaders who assume this role must be focused and developed. Your captains influence you and your team members for better or for worse. Therefore, I exhort each athletic program to consider implementing such a leadership development and training initiative through its athletic program. The benefits and the impact of such a program are far reaching and have immeasurable value.

While I believe leadership training has a lasting impact on players' lives long after their playing days are done, leadership training also has a direct effect on the immediate season. The type of team does not matter. When the game is ready to begin or when everything is on the line, when immediate motivational words and actions are required to fire up the team, you can almost always find an "engine" in the middle of the huddle, driving and compelling and pressing the team forward. That is the team leader! We see it in Ray Lewis of the Baltimore Ravens and Kevin Garnett of the Boston Celtics. Their effort, intensity, and high expectations for themselves give them the freedom to stand in the middle of the huddle and be the voice of the team.

Leadership is not for everyone, but everyone needs a leader to set a course to follow. Without a leader, the huddle is incomplete. If you are a leader you will be noticed. There is no need to ask to be a leader. Your character will reveal who you are and will attract or repel others. If it attracts, it is because your focus is off of self. True leadership is focused and rooted in love for God and others. If you lead from this perspective, people will be drawn to you and want to be led by you and will be open to your character affecting and growing their character. As your leadership resembles the life of Jesus and his selfless example, in time the individual characters in the huddle will begin to reflect his character as well. As a leader, you will be humbled to see that character has transferred, the team has been transformed, and the huddle has been changed forever.

PERSONAL EVALUATION/DISCUSSION QUESTIONS

1. Where have you seen positive team leadership within an athletic team? (Could be from high school, college, or professional sports.)

2. Name the individual(s) above and identify the traits or characteristics that made them successful.

3. What benefit did the team experience as a result of the player's leadership?

4. How would you and your team directly benefit from leadership training?

APPENDIX

Reflections from the Chattanooga Christian School Men's Varsity Soccer Players on the 2011 Season

Playing Soccer at CCS wasn't just a sport. It was worship of God. We trained and sacrificed our bodies for each other. In one sentence, our play was Soli Deo Gloria. Second to that was the huddle. It was more than just a place to get ready for the game; it was a place to bond and become brothers.

—**Sasha Peters**, #1, left midfielder

A band of brothers, working and striving toward a common goal—there is something to be said about that union, that fellowship. Not enough is said about the true bond that is formed when a group comes together and, through relentless effort, determination, and pursuit of a goal, achieves greatness. Our team was family. The season became a series of long, hard-fought battles that required each player to contribute his best. Our relationships with each other, the bond that was strengthened through trial after trial, practice after practice, game after game—that is what led us through to the end.

—**Nathan Boldt**, #18, defensive midfielder

The team was *strong.* We were not the strongest team physically or the most skilled, but we played with all of our hearts for each other, for our coach, and for the glory of God alone! I will always remember being able to look around the huddle and, regardless of our differences, know I was going to lay everything I had on the line for them and that they were going to do the same. Through this microcosm of life, we learned how to die to ourselves and find life in something bigger then ourselves. Soli Deo Gloria!

—**Roy Anderson**, #4, center back

We were more than just a soccer team that year. There was a chemistry within that group of guys that you cannot buy, for we were a band of brothers on and off the field. We understood that soccer was not life; however, each game was our opportunity to "get away" from everything else for ninety minutes and play the game we all passionately loved together. It united us. When we faced adversity, which we certainly did, we were able to overcome it *as a team* and achieve the goal we had set at the beginning of the season.

—**Taylor Black**, #11, center midfielder

I felt a strong sense of community, like a family. The camaraderie on our team is what made us state championship material. Throughout the journey God's hand was clearly on our team. The journey taught me hard work, perseverance, to play with heart, and to invest in people.

—**Tim Love**, #16, center midfielder

The most daunting challenges to our success were off the field. The dropping of our self-interests and submitting of ourselves to the good of the team were the most difficult and subsequently most rewarding things we accomplished throughout the course of that season. There were occasions when our team dynamics and unity had opportunities to deteriorate, but our common goal from the start was to play for the glory of Christ—and he saw fit to honor that in spite of our flaws.

—**Jacob Warren**, #5, defender

Coach really talked about the "huddle" a lot. The huddle was a way for us to prepare ourselves for what lay ahead, to ready our minds to do battle on that field. I grew very close to my team that season and will always remember the guys that I won state with. It was really amazing to see the way God brought us together after some struggles and defeats. Thank you, Coach, for everything you sacrificed for us. Thank you for investing so much of your time in us and teaching us to become godly men. Many of the things you said will stick with me forever.

—**Michael Powell**, #3, striker

The 2011 season was great for me because of the mentoring I received from older players. I really believe that as a result of that season I grew not only as a soccer player but more importantly overall as a person. I learned so many lessons from listening to what others had to say and noticing the examples they set for the team. I do not think I would be in quite the same position right now if not for that team.

—**Richard Reinink**, #14, center back

No matter the mistakes I made, the team, Coach Brower, and Coach Nelson always picked me up. The huddle is the perfect picture of what that year was: a brotherhood that cared more about the guys standing next to them than about the competitive life around us. We played for the brothers kneeling next to us and, in the end, it was for each other that we fought and sacrificed. The game was about more than a ball; it was about living life together through the ups and downs, learning to grow as a brotherhood.

—**Cameron Anderson**, goalie

Around the third game in, during a tournament in Atlanta, I tore my hamstring and was out for the season. This change might not have been what I wanted, but it was what God had planned for my life and was what I needed, because it allowed me to actually become a leader on the team instead of just leading through performance. The sideline gave me a different perspective, and instead of just trying to increase my own accolades, I was able to encourage my brothers and push them to stay focused on the mission. This change allowed me to become a better leader for life.

—**Rocklin Shumaker**, #2, striker

The 2011 soccer season was a great time in my life. Through the highs and lows of the season we remained focused on our creed, Soli Deo Gloria (Glory to God alone). Playing for God's glory is what drove us to be successful and have an amazing time doing it. Winning that State Championship is one of the proudest accomplishments of my life, but it pales in comparison to the experiences we had and relationships we forged that season. It was truly a blessing being on that team and an experience I will cherish forever.

—**Nick Russell, #21**, right midfielder

NOTES

Chapter One: Perspective Changes Everything!

1. *Chariots of Fire,* Warner Brothers Pictures, 1981; Warner Home Video, 1992.

2. Tim Tebow and Nathan Whitaker, *Through My Eyes,* (New York: Harper Collins, 2011), 173.

3. Ibid., 175.

4. Mike Yorkey, *Playing with Purpose: Tim Tebow, Jeremy Lin, and Today's Top Athletes* (Uhrichsville, OH: Barbour Publishing, 2012), 231.

5. S. L. Price, "The Curse of Brightness," *Sports Illustrated,* June 11, 2012, 44.

6. Yorkey, *Playing with Purpose,* 235.

7. Ibid., 234.

8. Jerry Crasnick, "Josh Hamilton Ups the Ante: His Four-Home Run Night Rewards His Faith—in Religion, His Skills and His Future," *ESPN,* May 2, 2012. http://espn.go.com/mlb/story/_/id/7907569/mlb-hamilton-4-hrs-raise-stakes-future.

9. Ibid.

10. "The Basketball Star No One Wanted: Jeremy Lin's Unlikely Triumph," Owen Strachan, *The Gospel Coalition,* February 13, 2012, thegospelcoalition.org/blogs/tgc/2012/02/13/the-basketball-star-no-one-wanted-jeremy-lins-unlikely-triumph.

11. "*Linsanity* continues as Lin proves he's no fluke in win over Lakers," Chris Mannix, *Sports Illustrated,* February 16, 2012, http://sportsillustrated.cnn.com/2012/writers/chris_mannix/02/11/jeremy.lin/index.html.

12. Quoted in "Jeremy Lin's Favorite Bible Verse Reflects His Story of Perseverance," Eryn Sun, *The Christian Post,* February 18, 2012,

http://www.christianpost.com/news/jeremy-lins-favorite-bible-verse
-reflects-his-story-of-perseverance-69781.

13. Ibid.

14. Elizabeth Tenety, "Faith, Sin and Jeremy Lin," *Washington Post*, February 17, 2012. http://www.washingtonpost.com/national
/on-faith/jeremy-lins-christian-side-his-pastor-and-spiritual-adviser
-speaks-out/2012/02/17/gIQAIkuwJR_story.html.

Stage One: Preseason

1. Theodore Roosevelt, "The Man in the Arena," *Almanac of Theodore Roosevelt,* accessed July 1, 2012, http://theodore-roosevelt.com
/images/research/speeches/maninthe arena.pdf.

2. "The Wizard's Wisdom: 'Woodenisms,'" ESPN.com staff, ESPN, June 4, 2010, http://sports.espn.go.com/ncb/news/story?id=5249709.

Chapter Two: Risk Your Best

1. Michael Mink, "Mia Hamm Set High Goals: Sure-Footed Competitor Gave America a Leg up on the Soccer Field," *Investor's Business Daily,* November 3, 2003; quoted in William J. O'Neal, *Sports Leaders and Success* (New York: McGraw-Hill, 2004), 7.

2. Ibid.

3. "Mia Hamm biography," A&E Networks, accessed February 12, 2013, http://www.biography.com/people/mia-hamm-16472547.

4. Ibid.

5. *NBA Encyclopedia: Playoff Edition*, http://www.nba.com/history
/players/jordan_stats.html.

6. "The Legs Feed the Wolf," *Miracle*, directed by Gavin O'Connor (2004; Burbank, CA: Buena Vista Home Entertainment, 2004), DVD.

7. Chris Warden, "Running Back Walter Payton: Determination Helped Him Run over Competition," *Investor's Business Daily,* November 8, 1999; quoted in O'Neal, *Sports Leaders and Success*, 100.

8. Ibid.

9. Theodore Roosevelt, "The Man in the Arena," *Almanac of Theodore Roosevelt,* accessed July 1, 2012, http://theodore-roosevelt.com
/images/research/speeches/maninthe arena.pdf.

Chapter Three: Selected

1. John C. Maxwell, *Developing the Leaders around You: How to Help Others Reach Their Full Potential* (Nashville, TN: Thomas Nelson, 1995), 144.

2. Mike Reiss, "Brady's Cinderella Story Never Gets Old: ESPN Documentary 'The Brady 6' Captures Quarterback's Defiant Rise to the Top," *ESPN*, April 12, 2011, http://sports.espn.go.com/boston/nfl/columns/story?columnist=reiss_mike&id=6303923.

3. Ibid.

4. Jeff Janssen, *Championship Team Building: What Every Coach Needs to Know to Build a Motivated, Committed and Cohesive Team* (Tucson, AZ: Winning the Mental Game, 1999), 93.

5. Nick Cafardo, "Opening Kickoff: Brady's emergence and a super season started Patriots' decade of dominance," The Boston Globe, January 29, 2012, http://www.boston.com/sports/football/patriots/articles/2012/01/29/remembering_the_patriots_first_super_bowl_win/.

6. "#12—Tom Brady," New England Patriots, accessed February 12, 2013, http://www.patriots.com/team/roster/Tom-Brady/272d4f2c-1bb9-4372-b02c-dfa3fa60575b.

7. ESPN.com staff, "The Wizard's Wisdom: 'Woodenisms,'" ESPN, June 4, 2010, http://sports.espn.go.com/ncb/news/story?id=5249709.

8. "No. 5: Lisa Leslie" in "Top 40 Female Athletes: Counting Down the Best of the Past 40 Years," Mechelle Voepel, accessed February 6, 2013, http://espn.go.com/espnw/title-ix/top-40-female-athletes/_/num/37.

Chapter Four: The Rules of Engagement

1. "Michael Vick biography," A&E Television Networks, accessed February 13, 2013, http://www.biography.com/people/michael-vick-241100.

2. Ibid.

3. Ibid.

4. Ibid.

5. Stephen Smith, "Michael Vick: 'I became better at reading dogs than reading defenses,'" *CBS News*, July 17, 2012, http://www.cbsnews.com/8301-31751_162-57473892-10391697/michael-vick-i-became-better-at-reading-dogs-than-reading-defenses/.

6. Ibid.

7. "Vick apologizes, asks for forgiveness in post-plea statement," Associated Press, August 28, 2007, http://sports.espn.go.com/nfl/news/story?id=2993103.

8. "God is in control," Mark Bergin, *WORLD*, December 3, 2010, http://www.worldmag.com/2010/12/god_is_in_control.

9. "Dan Hanzus, "Michael Vick's brother vents about Philadelphia Eagles," *NFL*, November 5, 2012, http://www.nfl.com/news/story/0ap1000000091088/article/michael-vicks-brother-vents-about-philadelphia-eagles.

10. "Lessons from the Dead," *Remember the Titans*, directed by Boaz Yakin (2000; Burbank, CA: Buena Vista Home Entertainment, 2004), DVD.

11. Ibid., "Setting the Rules."

12. Lee Jenkins, "Promise Keeper," *Sports Illustrated*, July 2, 2012, 38.

Chapter Five: So These Are My Teammates?

1. John C. Maxwell, *Talent Is Never Enough: Discover the Choices That Will Take You Beyond Your Talent* (Nashville, TN: Thomas Nelson, 2007) 262.

2. Phil Jackson, *Sacred Hoops: Spiritual Lessons of a Hardwood Warrior*, (New York: Hyperion, 2006), 6.

3. David L. Porter, *Michael Jordan: A Biography* (Westport, CN: Greenwood Publishing Group, 2007), 176.

4. *Secrets of SEAL Team Six*, documentary aired on the Discovery Channel, July 10, 2011.

Stage Two: Regular Season

1. Investor's Business Daily, *Sports Leaders and Success: 55 Top Sports Leaders and How They Achieved Greatness* (New York: McGraw-Hill, 2004), 33.

2. Jeff Janssen, *Championship Team Building: What Every Coach Needs to Know to Build a Motivated, Committed and Cohesive Team* (Tucson, AZ: Winning the Mental Game, 1999), 39.

Chapter Six: This *Is* "Next Year"

1. Jeff Janssen, *Championship Team Building: What Every Coach Needs to Know to Build a Motivated, Committed and Cohesive Team* (Tucson, AZ: Winning the Mental Game, 1999), 43.

2. John Wooden and Steve Jamison, *Wooden: A Lifetime of Observations and Reflections on and off the Court* (Lincolnwood, IL: Contemporary Publishing Company, 1997), 102.

3. John Wooden and Steve Jamison, *Wooden on Leadership: How to Create a Winning Organization* (New York: McGraw-Hill, 2005), 54.

4. Wooden and Jamison, *Wooden*, 87.

5. Pat Williams, Grant Hill, Michael Weinreb, and Doug Collins, *How to Be Like Mike: Life Lessons about Basketball's Best* (Deerfield Beach, FL: Healthy Communication, Inc., 2001), 61.

6. Ibid., 30–31.

7. Ibid., 29.

8. John Edmund Haggai, *The Influential Leader: 12 Steps to Igniting Visionary Decision Making* (Eugene, OR: Harvest House Publishers, 2009), 21–22.

9. Ibid., 27.

10. Tommy Newberry, *Success Is Not an Accident* (Carol Stream, IL: Tyndale House, 2007), 57.

11. "On the Team," *Rudy*, directed by David Anspaugh, (1993; Culver City, CA: TriStar Pictures, 1993), DVD.

12. Wooden and Jamison, *Wooden on Leadership*, 197.

13. *Rudy*, "Two Quitters," DVD.

Chapter Seven: Pressing On

1. "Big Shadows," *Rocky Balboa*, directed by Sylvester Stallone, (2006; Metro-Goldwyn-Mayer [MGM], Columbia Pictures, Revolution Studios, 2006), DVD.

2. John Wooden and Steve Jamison, *Wooden: A Lifetime of Observations and Reflections on and off the Court* (Lincolnwood, IL: Contemporary Publishing Company, 1997), 150.

3. "Don't Quit," http://www.essentiallifeskills.net/itcouldbedone.html.

Chapter Eight: Shoot Straight with Me

1. Nicholas Bragg, "Effective Communication in Sports," *Livestrong.com*, September 2, 2010, http://www.livestrong.com/article/220761-effective-communication-in-sports/.

Chapter Nine: Winning the Head Game

1 Grant Wahl, "The World's Team," *Sports Illustrated*, October 8, 2012, 71.

2. "Thinking," Walter D. Wintle, quoted on Good Reads, http://www.goodreads.com/quotes/327729-if-you-think-you-are-beaten -you-are-if-you.

3. "Breaking Down the Barriers in Your Mind," Nigel Risner, accessed February 6, 2012, http://career.cabalgroup.com/Articles /MIH/barriers.htm.

4. Alan Goldberg, *Playing Out of Your Mind*, (Spring City, PA: Reedswain, 1997), 9.

Chapter Ten: Defined in Battle

1. Gabriel Baumgaertner, "An Oral History of the Infamous 1997 Holyfield-Tyson 'Bite Fight,'" *Sports Illustrated*, posted June 29, 2012, http://sportsillustrated.cnn.com/2012/writers/the_bonus/06/28 /tyson-holyfield-oral-history/index.html.

2. "Zinedine Zidane headbutt statue unveiled in Paris," France 24, September 26, 2012, http://www.france24.com/en/20120926-france-art -football-world-cup-2006-zidane-headbutt-statue-paris-pompidou-centre.

3. ESPN.com News Services, "Suspensions without Pay, Won't Be Staggered," *ESPN*, http://sports.espn.go.com/nba/news/story?id=1928540.

4. "Elizabeth Lambert, the hair-pulling college soccer player, is back after serving two-game suspension," Andy Clayton, NY Daily News, August 28, 2010, http://www.nydailynews.com/sports/college /elizabeth-lambert-hair-pulling-college-soccer-player-back-serving -two-game-suspension-article-1.206471.

5. Christopher Santarelli, "How Did Tim Tebow Respond to Critic Telling Him to Tone down Jesus Talk?" *The Blaze*, November 22, 2011, http://www.theblaze.com/stories/how-did-tim-tebow-respond -to-critic-telling-him-to-tone-down-jesus-talk/.

6. Nate Davis, "Jets, Broncos Finally Complete Deal for Tim Tebow," *USA Today: The Huddle*, March 22, 2012, http://content .usatoday.com/communities/thehuddle/post/2012/03 /report-jets-acquire-tim-tebow-from-broncos-for-fourth-round -draft-pick/1.

7. Ibid.

Stage Three: Playoffs

1. Michael Jordan and Mark Vancil, *I Can't Accept Not Trying* (San Francisco: Harper, 1994).

2. Ibid.

Chapter Eleven: Collective Separation

1. Scott Burnside, "Kings Owe Cup Run to Tight Group," *ESPN*, June 12, 2012, http://espn.go.com/nhl/playoffs/2012/story/_/id /8040057/los-angeles-kings-pulled-together-right-time-way-their -first-stanley-cup-win.

2. "The Ubuntu story," accessed February 13, 2012, http://www .ubuntu.com/project/about-ubuntu.

3. Lee Jenkins, "The Iceman Cometh," *Sports Illustrated*, June 25, 2012, 47.

4. Ibid., 48.

5. Ibid., 47.

6. Lee Jenkins, "Promise Keeper," *Sports Illustrated*, July 2, 2012, 38.

7. Ibid.

8. Ibid.

9. Lee Jenkins, "The Iceman Cometh," 47.

10. Ibid.

11. Ibid.

12. Ibid., 50.

13. Ibid., 51.

14. David Epstein and Jon Wertheim, "Rhiannon Hull," *Sports Illustrated*, March 12, 2012, 58-62.

15. Ibid., 60.

16. Ibid., 61.

Chapter Twelve: Staying on Center

1. Peter King, "Way out of Bounds," *Sports Illustrated*, March 12, 2012, 40.

2. Ibid.

3. "New Orleans Saints Face the Consequences of Bounty Allegations," *The Moody Standard*, April 18, 2012, http://www.moody standard.com/new-orleans-saints-bounty-allegations/.

4. Knox Bardeen, "Roger Goodell's Punishment for Saints Bounty Program Is Far Too Weak," *Bleacher Report*, May 2, 2012, http://bleacherreport.com/articles/1169933-roger-goodells -punishment-for-saints-bounty-program-is-far-too-weak.

5. Tom Verducci, "Ten Years After," *Sports Illustrated*, June 4, 2012, 49.

6. Ibid., 51.

Chapter Thirteen: Victory in Defeat

1. "U.S. Men's Soccer Beats Mexico In Mexico For 1st Time: Michael Orozco Fiscal Scores Game-Winning Goal," Michael Weissenstein, *Huffington Post*, August 15, 2012, http://www.huffington post.com/2012/08/15/us-soccer-mexico-1-0-michael-orozco-goal -video_n_1786135.html.

2. Leif H. Smith, Sports Psychology for Dummies (Mississauga, ON: John Wiley and Sons, 2010), 183.

3. Ibid.

4. Chad Bonham, *Excellence: The Heart and Soul in Sports* (Venture, CA: Regal, 2009), 147.

5. Jim Trotter, "Why?" *Sports Illustrated*, May 14, 2012, 45.

6. Alexander Wolff, "Technical Knockout," *Sports Illustrated*, April 12, 1993, http://sportsillustrated.cnn.com/vault/article/magazine /MAG1138253/index.htm.

7. B. C. Forbes Quotes, *ThinkExist.com*, http://thinkexist.com/quo tation/history-has-demonstrated-that-the-most-notable/1634516 .html. Accessed November 13, 2012.

Chapter Fifteen: Championships

1. Chris Chase, "Terrell Suggs Goes out of His Way to Bash Tim Tebow," *Yahoo! Sports*, January 3, 2012, http://sports.yahoo.com/nfl /blog/shutdown_corner/post/Terrell-Suggs-goes-out-of-his-way -to-bash-Tim-Te?urn=nfl-wp15161.

2. Mike Florio, "Suggs on Tebow: 'We Don't Need God on Our Sidelines,' " *NBC Sports*, January 4, 2012, http://profootballtalk.nbcsports.com/2012/01/04/suggs-on-tebow-we-dont-need-god-on-our-sidelines/.

3. "Gabby Douglas Praises God; Christian Gymnast Thankful After Winning All-Around Gold at Olympics 2012," Daniel Blake, *The Christian Post*, August 2, 2012, http://global.christianpost.com/news/gabby-douglas-praises-god-christian-gymnast-thankful-after-winning-all-around-gold-at-olympics-2012-79386/.

4. Ibid.

5. "Gabby Douglas More Popular Than Michael Phelps With NBC Olympics Audience," Nicola Menzie, *The Christian Post*, August 7, 2012, http://www.christianpost.com/news/gabby-douglas-more-popular-than-michael-phelps-with-nbc-olympics-audience-79637/

6. Tim Tebow and Nathan Whitaker, *Through My Eyes*, (New York: Harper Collins, 2011), 123.

7. Ibid., 124.

Stage Four: Post-Season

1. John Wooden and Steve Jamison, *Wooden on Leadership: How to Create a Winning Organization* (New York: McGraw-Hill, 2005), 43.

Chapter Sixteen: For Life

1. Ian Thomsen, "Last Stand of the Big Three," *Sports Illustrated*, June 4, 2012, 61.